An Introduction to Carp Fishing

An Introduction to Carp Fishing

David Batten

The Crowood Press

First published in 1989 by
The Crowood Press Ltd
Ramsbury, Marlborough
Wiltshire SN8 2HR

Paperback edition 1994

British Library Cataloguing-in-Publication Data
A catalogue record for this book is
available from the British Library.

ISBN 1 85223 817 8

Typeset by PCS Typesetting, Frome, Somerset.
Printed and bound in Great Britain by
BPC Hazell Books Ltd
A member of
The British Printing Company Ltd

Contents

Acknowledgements

Despite any book being the author's own work, so much of what he may write about is bound to have been influenced by contact with many others up to the point of putting pen to paper. It will not have been apparent at the particular moment in time that a contribution was made, but later when there is time to reflect we all recognise that we were influenced or guided by friends and contacts in all walks in life. With this in mind it is only fair that I personally express my thanks to all those who may have influenced my directions in angling and in the writing of this series of books.

Particular mention must be made of those who have directly helped with material, physical and psychological support during the many months spent researching, writing and illustrating, times when it seemed impossible that everything would come to fruition. My greatest thanks must go to my wife Kathy who has had the task of preparing the manuscripts, indexes and turning out at all hours of the night to help get some photographs for the book, and generally putting up with an angler who has not been able to go fishing as and when he wished!

For their photographic contributions, my thanks go to Colin Brett, Chris Turnbull and John Wilson. Some special mention is due to John who, in the midst of his own pressures of filming and writing, gave up precious time to take photographs on the coldest day of summer, for the cover of the book! Thanks also to Mike Wood for his assistance in getting photographic material and references for the illustrations, and for his pleasant company on many successful and not so successful sessions!

Introduction

Whatever your reason for picking up this book, be it to understand how to get on the first rung of the ladder to carp fishing success or perhaps to observe and take stock of your own understanding and ability (or maybe lack of it!) you will find in the following pages all the advice you need for successful carp fishing.

Whether your interest in carp fishing has recently arisen from the enthusiasm of others, perhaps friends have been successful and you now wish to try it yourself, or whether your early success has been short-lived and you are now struggling to catch, help is now at hand.

So much has happened in the last couple of years with bait and tackle developments, that it is possible just to buy some of the latest ready-made baits, use the latest rig and catch almost instantly, particularly if you follow the lead of a successful carp angler on your chosen water. If you move into the swim when he leaves and cast your bait where he did, it is almost guaranteed that you will catch. Only when the bites stop will you be lost: should you choose another bait, flavour, rig or swim?

It is not possible for me to give you instant skills of watercraft but you will gain an understanding of it which will encourage you to develop your own techniques. You will certainly need to try to improve your skills, as you may well spend a great deal of time coming to terms with the complex issue of catching what on many waters are now *educated* carp! On just about every water throughout the country, pressure has led to the carp becoming wary of many baits, methods and combinations of both. To stand any chance of succeeding on some of these waters it will not only be necessary to have an understanding of the latest bait or method, but also to be able to predict the behaviour of your quarry in a given situation, an ability that will come with experience. The following chapters should guide you along the right path.

The time will arrive when you catch consistently under a variety of situations, even the most difficult. It is again very easy once successful to fall into the one method, one bait syndrome with the disastrous result that you stop catching without really knowing why. Think hard, take stock of your thoughts and reread the following chapters!

1 *The Species*

Although many anglers pursue carp as their primary species, some dedicating *all* their time to this single species, not every angler will understand fully certain characteristics of the various strains of the species. The following chapter will supply the basic background and history of our quarry. For those who wish to know more about the species some recommended reading is listed in the reference section at the end of this book.

Of those anglers who are taking up carp fishing and those who have many years' experience behind them, it is highly likely that few will have fished for, let alone hooked, played and landed, the original strain of carp (illustrated in Fig 1) that led the way to the specially cultivated strains we now have the opportunity to fish for. Those who have fished for and been successful in hooking, playing and landing the original 'wild' strain of carp, will all admit to the surprise of how small the fish actually is, after experiencing a fight which is usually nothing short of spectacular and which gives the impression of having hooked a much bigger fish. Few of the true 'wild' strain grow beyond ten pounds in weight, although some waters may hold fish in excess of this. Most wild carp waters are grossly overstocked, thereby restricting growth to around two to three pounds in many of the waters still holding them. When using light tackle the fight can be as described – spectacular – so if the opportunity comes your way, seize it, grasp the experience and enjoy some sport which will probably die out in future years. Unfortunately, few fisheries seem interested in stocking 'wildies', and some even frown on them.

These original wild fish were imported into England somewhere between the thirteenth and fifteenth centuries. Different authorities list different periods but the important fact is they were undoubtedly introduced by monks coming from the Continent. The monks used the humble carp as a major part of their diet and wherever they settled and built their monasteries, they also built stew ponds, specially to grow and hold stocks of carp for food.

Carp became more popular not for their sporting qualities, but for the production of faster-growing strains to hasten the process of getting fish to a suitable size for table use in restaurants, etc., on the Continent, particularly in the northern countries of Germany, Hungary and Czechoslovakia. At the same time there came a genetic development that saw the early, fully scaled, common-type carp replaced by successive genetic cultivations of the numerous mirror carp variations through to the scale-free leather carp, all of which again aided table preparation by excluding scales.

This development was, however, to have its benefits in angling, as these table fish were being imported into the English fish farms to supply the many European families resident in England. Ultimately these fish were interbred and new strains cultivated and eventually introduced for stocking into various waters such as fisheries like Redmire,

Two generations of wild carp: a bright young fish and the darker tones of an older specimen.

Above: A young wild common carp from a
Norfolk mere.

Below: The distinctive scale pattern on a gravel-
pit 18lb mirror carp.

Fig 1 Common carp

culminating in record-weight fish, firstly Dick Walker's forty-four pounds common and then Chris Yates' fifty-one pound six ounce mirror. Both of these carp would have descended from those Continental imports.

All these strains belong to the same species of *Cyprinus carpio*, with the exception of the crucian carp which is *Carassius carassius* (*see* Fig 2). Whether the fish are fully scaled, partly scaled or leather, they are all related to each other. However, there is a different classification of names related to where they were cultivated, and these various names can indicate just what sort of fish you may be likely to catch. The original strain was the 'Galician', which originated in Poland. It is probably the most evenly proportioned of the

numerous strains and is the strain of fish stocked into Redmire. A more recently introduced strain today is the Dinkelsbuehler from Germany which is a more rounded, plump-looking fish.

While the introduction of many of today's fish took place many years ago and we are able to delight in the pleasure of catching good mirror and leather carp, a phenomenon is taking place on waters that are old enough, of remission to more fully scaled common carp. If the water in question is stocked only with mirrors this process is very slow, but the genetic change that gives us mirror and leather carp is recessive, and over a very long period even the successful offspring of each generation will slip slowly back towards

Fig 2   Crucian carp

being fully scaled again. With an introduction of the fully scaled wild strain into a stock of mirror carp the process will see a swift return to the fully scaled variety, a reason why the 'wild' carp is not so popular, particularly in big carp waters. There is no reason why they should not be held in fisheries though, as the phenomenon is limited to waters where carp breed, and very few English waters actually breed their own fry due to water temperatures being too unstable.

Spawning usually takes place in May or June and is dependent on the water temperature reaching and maintaining 20°C (68°F), long enough to allow a successful session. Too often we witness the carp on most waters 'going through the motions'

without success due to the variable English weather, although some southern waters with their slightly higher temperatures do get a higher success rate.

Before closing this chapter, there is one more species of carp that should be included and that is the crucian carp, *Carassius carassius*. By comparison with the aforementioned king strains these might seem small, with a record weight of five pounds ten ounces, and most average fish seem to weigh between one and two pounds. Fish upward of this weight are rare and to be treasured as they are splendid to fish for and to catch. Their shy habits make for a real test on some days (*see* Fig 3).

Many crucian waters suffer from over-

A golden-scaled crucian carp from a Norfolk mere.

stocking and stunting. Crucians spawn readily as a species and when in a mix with wild or common carp interbreed to a hybridisation giving them a 'wildie' common appearance with a longer body shape, a longer dorsal fin and stunted or fewer barbules. Although not a desirable strain, this is a very active sporty fish. Again, as with 'wildies', crucian carp are a valuable species and deserve more attention than many carp anglers bother to give them. Get amongst them with float tackle if you can and you will enjoy it as much as the other species!

Left: Mike Woods with fine examples of crucian and wild carp from a Norfolk mere.

The torpedo shape of a near 'wildie' common carp weighing in at 16lb 6oz.

15

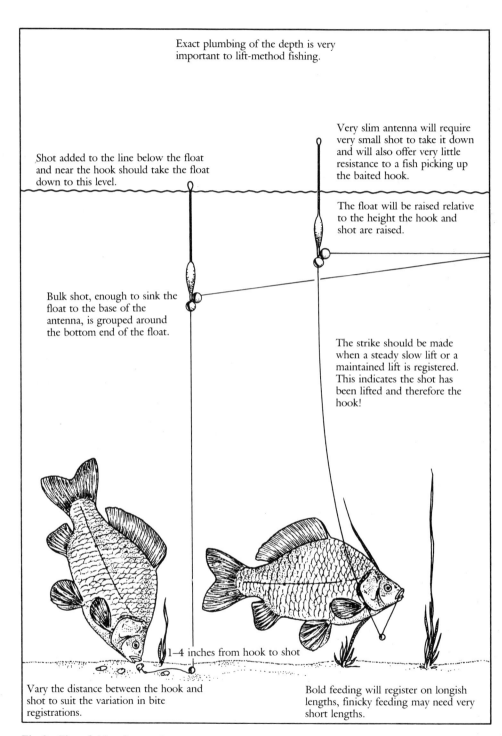

Exact plumbing of the depth is very important to lift-method fishing.

Shot added to the line below the float and near the hook should take the float down to this level.

Very slim antenna will require very small shot to take it down and will also offer very little resistance to a fish picking up the baited hook.

The float will be raised relative to the height the hook and shot are raised.

Bulk shot, enough to sink the float to the base of the antenna, is grouped around the bottom end of the float.

The strike should be made when a steady slow lift or a maintained lift is registered. This indicates the shot has been lifted and therefore the hook!

1–4 inches from hook to shot

Vary the distance between the hook and shot to suit the variation in bite registrations.

Bold feeding will register on longish lengths, finicky feeding may need very short lengths.

Fig 3   Float fishing for crucian carp

2 Fisheries

TYPES OF FISHERY

Today's anglers have access to a far greater variety of types of carp fishery than has been available before. This range includes small farm ponds, estate lakes, gravel and clay pits, ornamental lakes and many more types of enclosed water – in fact any piece of water can with careful consideration be made into a carp fishery.

Carp fisheries fall into perhaps three categories. The first is the club water where carp are introduced by club officials who want to offer a wide range of species for their members to catch. The second is the commercial fishery that aims to offer good quality fishing on a joint season and day ticket basis, where higher levels of carp stocks are introduced to generate a wider interest for the sort of anglers who will pay for good, quality fishing. Some syndicate waters fall into this category as well, and these are usually ones where high quality fishing for several different species is available, and where the growing on of large carp is secondary and a bonus feature for the future. The third category is the carp syndicate water, the main reason for its existence being to grow carp to the biggest possible size, to give above average quality carp fishing to a small number of dedicated carp anglers.

All three categories have something to offer, but to varying degrees. The club-owned or leased water which may be heavily stocked with carp to cater for the needs of club anglers, offers easy-to-catch fish; the need for this is vital to the success of the club as poorly stocked waters result in poorly supported clubs. This fact overcomes some club officials who presume that the more fish there are the greater the support for the club will be. This is true, but the heavy stockings of carp can be a mixed blessing: they will certainly provide easy fishing for club anglers and allow an easy introduction to carp fishing but it is likely that this type of water will quickly become uninteresting and new locations and fisheries will be sought.

Fish in well-stocked or possibly over-stocked waters may never reach the size everybody hopes they will, due to lack of food and nutrients. Competition for the given amount of food available will be out of balance and fish of all species will reach only the size their environment will allow, with some species being overrun or even wiped out by the pressure from a large species like carp. If the water is a club fishery and perhaps the club's only water, the heavy stocking with carp might actually be to the detriment of the club and many of its less intense members.

There will always be the type of fishery with a small, hungry, overstocked water where the fish will range from about five pounds up to a ceiling of twelve or thirteen pounds, with perhaps the odd fish of fifteen to sixteen pounds. On the other hand there will be the big, sparsely stocked water, where it is hard to locate fish and equally hard to catch them, that will probably be beyond most beginners' or even average carp anglers' ability. This type of water will probably produce big carp from

Simon Ladd with a netful of future heavyweights ready for stocking into the growing-on pond.

Taverham No. 3 gravel pit, home of some very large mirror carp.

Close season preparation of an estate lake fishery growing-on pond by syndicate members.

Fig 4   Estate lake

Fig 5   Gravel pit

around twenty-five pounds up to the possible record-breaking weight of fifty-one pounds six ounces or maybe more – very good, but the sort of water to destroy the faint hearted and inexperienced!

Between these two extreme examples there is a fishery that will give satisfaction to everybody, from the casual angler who would like to catch the occasional carp through to the newcomer to carp fishing and on through the various levels of commitment to carp fishing to the dedicated, big fish only, carp angler. This will be a balanced and controlled fishery where stocking levels and environmental conditions are monitored and controlled by fishery managers, owners and club officials. They will have to limit the level of stocks of fish to gain their optimum growth potential while also maintaining their health. The two go hand in hand as only healthy fish grow, and they will be more likely to survive when there is a slight imbalance in their environment due perhaps to adverse climatic conditions.

STOCK CONTROL

The controlling of fish stocks may mean reducing the numbers of fish to maintain the best biomass levels. Assessed by weight of fish per acre, this means that you can, for example, have two hundred pounds of fish per acre in a reasonably rich water with twenty fish of ten pounds each, or ten fish at twenty pounds each, or even two hundred, one pound fish per acre. These weights and quantities must be subdivided by the species the water might contain, for example, roach, rudd, tench, carp and perch. It is important to have a mixture of species with different feeding requirements, including surface- and mid-water-feeding species like rudd and roach. These will not make heavy demands on the food reserves required by predominantly

bottom-feeding species like tench and carp.

With the balanced-fishery approach you can cultivate a water that will supply good fishing with all the mentioned species growing to their optimum weight. If the stocking levels are calculated slightly short of the maximum weight of fish per acre to allow for good growth, some carp will have a chance to grow into their upper weight potential, possibly to as large as twenty pounds and maybe even more, to satisfy all the various types of angler. It is the stock levels, no matter what sort or size of fishery you look at, that will decide on how good or bad a fishery is: too many fish in a small fishery can be as bad as too few in a large fishery.

There is no reason why a fishery should not contain only carp. Many fisheries exist that are stocked exclusively with carp or at least as near as they can be, either by initial design or by stocking levels slowly excluding existing stocks of other species. It really depends on whether you want purely carp fishing.

FINDING A GOOD CARP FISHERY

To start with, you would be well advised to locate and investigate a well-stocked, maybe overstocked carp fishery, if one exists in your area. Most areas of the country seem to have one commercially run carp fishery that will fit this bill! The only way to learn anything about bait presentation and tactics is to be catching carp regularly; if you are not able to catch on this sort of fishery you must be doing something wrong.

What types of water make good carp fisheries? Every carp angler will have his own idea of what makes a good or excellent carp fishery, but this opinion will be related in many cases to where that particular angler finds most success and maybe where his biggest fish came from; it could be this was

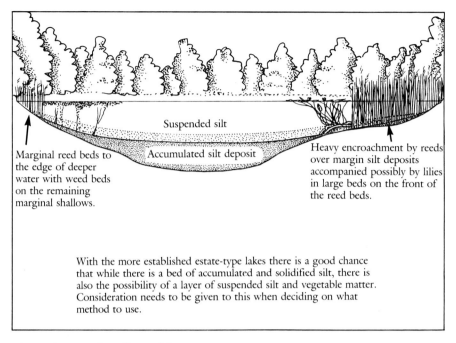

Suspended silt

Accumulated silt deposit

Marginal reed beds to
the edge of deeper
water with weed beds
on the remaining
marginal shallows.

Heavy encroachment by reeds
over margin silt deposits
accompanied possibly by lilies
in large beds on the front of
the reed beds.

With the more established estate-type lakes there is a good chance
that while there is a bed of accumulated and solidified silt, there is
also the possibility of a layer of suspended silt and vegetable matter.
Consideration needs to be given to this when deciding on what
method to use.

Fig 6   Cross-section of estate lake

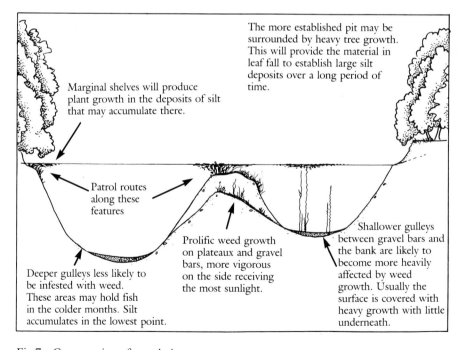

Marginal shelves will produce
plant growth in the deposits of silt
that may accumulate there.

The more established pit may be
surrounded by heavy tree growth.
This will provide the material in
leaf fall to establish large silt
deposits over a long period of
time.

Patrol routes
along these
features

Prolific weed growth
on plateaux and gravel
bars, more vigorous
on the side receiving
the most sunlight.

Shallower gulleys
between gravel bars and
the bank are likely to
become more heavily
affected by weed
growth. Usually the
surface is covered with
heavy growth with little
underneath.

Deeper gulleys less likely to
be infested with weed.
These areas may hold fish
in the colder months. Silt
accumulates in the lowest point.

Fig 7   Cross-section of gravel pit

The view towards a hot spot on an Essex gravel pit.

a small estate-type fishery (Fig 6) or a gravel-pit fishery (Fig 7). This tends to bias most of us into fishing confidently on *our* type of fishery and thinking that this is probably the best type of fishery – it is human nature!

The type of fishery to look for is the one that is close enough for you to be able to fish it frequently and get to know it well. This will give you the best results as you will learn how and when is the best moment to fish it, i.e. at what time of day and in what weather conditions it will and will not produce fish. The sort of carp fishing to look for should be related to your experience and you must learn to walk before you run; the weekly 'tackle for sale' columns are testimony to the many who fail by attempting the summit in their first season!

To find a good, well-stocked fishery ask a good tackle dealer. He should be able to suggest a local day ticket or club fishery that will give you the opportunity to get amongst the carp. Fisheries vary from small, maybe secluded, man-made pools of say one or two acres, to gravel pits in excess of one to two hundred acres. Each fishery will have features with similar characteristics, though they will vary in scale: shallow areas, deep areas, bars, snags and margins, etc. Each feature will present different problems, and observation of fish activity will be easier on the smaller fisheries. Also, those same activities studied on the small fishery will be of value when moving on to the intermediate-sized fishery and eventually the larger fishery, which might be your ultimate goal!

The main thing to remember is *not* to jump around from fishery to fishery, but to reap the benefits of the experience you gain. Once you have gained some sound experience, you can progress onwards to perhaps the nearer big fish waters and in due course move out to try the more widely known big fish waters throughout the UK and Europe.

3 *Location and Feeding Habits*

LOCATION OF CARP IN SUMMER

Having made your choice of water on which you hope to catch your first or maybe your next carp, your first move on arrival should be to leave the tackle in your car and take a slow walk around the whole water to get to know its make-up. This will be of more benefit than just dropping your tackle into the nearest swim and casting out your baits. Admittedly you can probably observe the water from your chosen swim but you will not learn any of its intimate secrets by looking at it from a distance, with or without binoculars.

The activity of feeding is generally related to the most productive location of food. This may vary at different times of the season but it is vital to remember that the deepest channel or section of water on a given lake or pit is most likely to hold the lowest concentrations of natural food items as the development of all aquatic life is dependent on light and temperature. Shallow lakes and pits produce more usable food than deep gravel pits, clay pits and quarries. (The margins and bars on these last three types of fishery are the most likely food producing and holding areas.) The shallowest, weediest areas of any water usually hold the highest concentration of natural foods in the form of snails, shrimps, beetles and various larvae.

The many successful carp anglers who catch carp regularly around the country have undoubtedly come to terms with fish location and within a short time discover the optimum swim. Many of these successful anglers actually locate carp with what could now be called a sixth sense, but really it is a finely cultivated form of water craft. It is acquired by combining natural instinct with methodical research into fish activities over many seasons, allied with regular fish catches to prove that all this was worthwhile!

This aptitude will come hard to some as it is not a natural part of their approach to angling as a whole. To any inquisitive or inspired angler who seeks to understand more, a walk round the lake is essential, be it two acres or two hundred acres, as this is the only way to observe the visible features. On the bigger waters it might be advisable to break these into smaller sections, as illustrated in Fig 8, which you can observe and fish more the way you would a small fishery.

Do not fall into the trap of fishing swims only where you have seen fish caught, for you are already too late. Look for feeding areas and fish them; the carp may never have seen a bait in the chosen area and take your baits confidently straight away and throughout the season! The location of weed beds, islands, shallows, visible bars, channels, bays, etc., is important as all of these may come into play at various times of the day and in various conditions. Once you are walking you should look for signs of carp that may be showing themselves by rolling or swimming near the

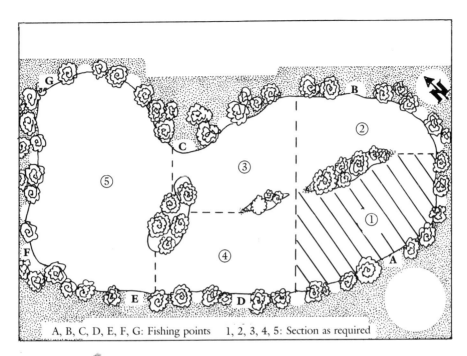

A, B, C, D, E, F, G: Fishing points   1, 2, 3, 4, 5: Section as required

Fig 8   Sections of lake

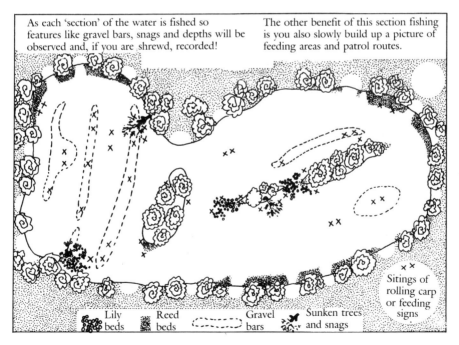

As each 'section' of the water is fished so features like gravel bars, snags and depths will be observed and, if you are shrewd, recorded!

The other benefit of this section fishing is you also slowly build up a picture of feeding areas and patrol routes.

Lily beds   Reed beds   Gravel bars   Sunken trees and snags   Sitings of rolling carp or feeding signs

Fig 9   Features on lake

Close season observation on a large estate lake.

The hot spot on a Norfolk club, gravel-pit carp fishery.

surface. On bright days they may be located close to or under weed beds, lily pads, and fallen trees. Take time and watch these in the warm, bright days for tell-tale signs of weed or leaf-stem movements. These may not be feeding areas but places of comfort where the carp can retreat to and feel safe, and which might supply some surface fishing with floating baits on days which might otherwise fail to produce any activity on bottom baits in open water.

On weed beds and lily beds the carp will look for and feed on suspended or natural food items that have accumulated as a result of wind and current action, and on larvae and snails, etc., which have taken up residence at certain times of the year. Weed bed and lily bed activities can be heard at night as carp suck items of food off the underside of surface leaves, etc. The sound is a very distinctive 'cloop'! (*See* Fig 9.)

Close season is a good time to do some research as you can combine the observation

with plumbing the depth with rod and line to confirm the contours of the bottom, revealing the locations of gravel bars, plateaux, etc., without the distraction of trying to catch fish. The finest way to achieve this is with an echo sounder if the use of boats is allowed on the chosen water. Some clubs may prohibit this, so check first, but some clubs may be grateful for this sort of record or maybe even have a chart of depths and features. It might pay to ask a club official at an early stage. A couple of hours' work with an echo sounder can reveal all the information which could take a whole season to accumulate using rod and line plumbing.

The location of possible features that may be patrol or feeding areas is important to any angler and of utmost importance if you wish to be consistently successful at catching carp. If you can, amongst all the possible areas, locate a feeding area or areas, you will be more likely to catch than if you just chuck and chance it. The carp is a master of its

At all times be observant and keep a watch for signs of activity over as much of the water as possible. Move or recast if consistent fish activity is noted in one area.

Fig 10   Observation – seated

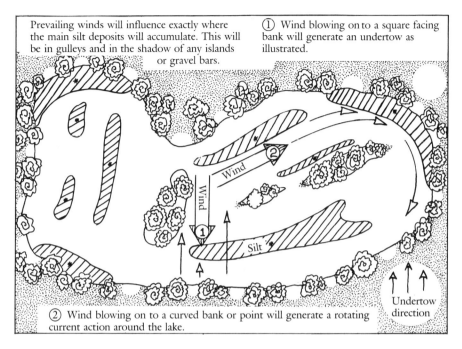

Prevailing winds will influence exactly where the main silt deposits will accumulate. This will be in gulleys and in the shadow of any islands or gravel bars.

① Wind blowing on to a square facing bank will generate an undertow as illustrated.

② Wind blowing on to a curved bank or point will generate a rotating current action around the lake.

Undertow direction

Fig 11 Wind on lake

environment and it will know where to feed at all times of the year and in various conditions, dictated by weather – mainly the wind. You must get to know the same things to give you maximum opportunities.

Everything may seem natural and permanent but in certain conditions changes take place; these changes should be exploited, so knowledge of the water being fished is paramount. Wind, as already stated, probably has the greatest influence on the carp's feeding activity as it generates surface movement towards one of the banks around the lake and the edge of any islands. It generates wave action on the facing margins which will release and stir up food items and debris from the bottom and the weed beds, colouring and flavouring the water. If the wind is strong enough and blows for a long enough period, an undertow is generated and

this release of material will be carried away from the bank; carp sensing this will exploit this food. If gravel bars and weed beds exist away from the bank these will also receive some of this turbulent disturbance and release of material, so again if you know they exist these areas can be fished at the right times (*see* Fig 11).

By the same token, still conditions have the effect of encouraging fish to frequent certain areas of a lake, particularly in bright, warm periods. It could be in the deeper areas that they find cooler water or in the shade of weed beds or lily beds where oxygen levels may be higher. This is another feature of wind-blown margins where the waves increase the oxygen content of the water. Observation of fish activity in given conditions on each individual water will allow a useful picture to build up in the angler's mind of which water

Above: The classic lines of a gravel-pit, scattered-scale mirror carp of 19lb.

Below: Classic lines of a gravel-pit 22lb mirror carp supported by Des Richardson.

Darren Cowle with an evening-caught 9lb leather carp from a club water.

Larger-sized bubbles in repeated
quantities in one area usually
indicate natural gas releases.

Large patches of small-sized bubbles
which seem to 'fizz' on the surface
usually indicate bottom-feeding fish.

A foraging and feeding carp may leave a
long trail of 'fizzy' bubbles along the
surface and there may be some clouding
or discolouration of the water.

Large or small areas of coloured water
may be the result of silt being put into
suspension by foraging and feeding carp.
Small species do create the same
circumstances, but one sure fact is these
areas are definite feeding areas!

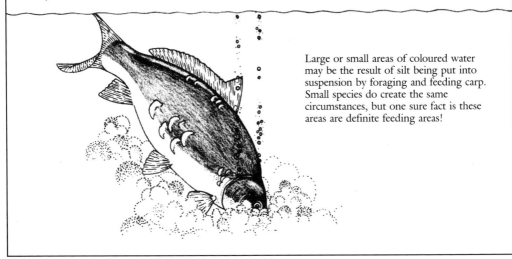

Fig 12   Clouding and bubbling from feeding carp

to fish, or where on a particular water to place a bait.

The location of feeding fish will depend on the visible forms of activity, which can be clouding of the water, large patches of bubbles or signs of fish rolling over a certain area, although this phenomenon is not a definite feeding indicator! The gullies that run between or beside gravel bars and islands are the likely places to witness clouding and bubbling as silt usually gets deposited in these areas as a result of the wind action described earlier. This silt is the place to find a high degree of natural food in the form of blood worm and other larvae forms. Weed beds usually form on the shallower silt deposits, increasing the natural food supply with swan mussels and invertebrates which can again be shaken free by wind action and undertows.

Shallow areas on some of the man-made lakes or on the gravel pits which are silty and weedy are also places to look for this clouding and bubbling. Mornings and evenings are ideal times to observe this close-in feeding particularly if bank-side disturbance is kept to a minimum.

If you are fortunate enough to be able to fish a quiet water it is worthwhile spending time checking for feeding activity in the margins and on the margins of any islands. On bank-side margins many food items get deposited by anglers and by the wind; carp will patrol these areas to exploit any opportunity that will present them with easy feeding, and if you are clever you in turn can exploit this to enhance your success, particularly during the hours of darkness (*see* Fig 12).

LOCATION OF CARP IN WINTER

There was a feeling amongst early carp anglers that fishing for carp during winter months was a waste of time as the carp hibernated and that they were only truly active in the warm summer months. This left only three to four months of the year in which they could be fished for and caught!

However, the increased interest in the species during the late sixties and early seventies saw the more dedicated carp anglers trying to catch carp in winter when the weather conditions were suitable, and succeeding, much to many people's surprise. The essential element in success was location; far from hibernating, the fish were to be found migrating to areas of the fisheries which offer suitable conditions for feeding, etc., during winter months. If you can locate these areas there is every chance, if you are prepared to work at it, that you can catch carp throughout the winter whenever conditions are not too severe.

If location forms the primary part of winter carp fishing, then bait and a consistent, regular feeding programme constitute the secondary part. If bait is placed into the holding area throughout the autumn and into the winter, there is every possibility that the carp will become dependent upon it. The best way to do this consistently is for two or more anglers to work as a team to bait and fish a known area. In many cases some of the fish caught are at their heaviest annual weights, making the effort all the more rewarding. Volumes of bait introduced need to be reduced to a level where the carp are not over feeding but looking for just a little bit more – the hook bait! Good-quality baits are essential at this time with attractors boosted to work better in the cold water.

To summarise on the subject of location and feeding habits, no matter what the type of water you are going to fish, you must apply some basic, logical thought to the location of your quarry. They need to feed, and they will seek out the most abundant and easy-to-obtain supply; it is up to you to locate likely features that promote the right conditions in which natural food supplies flourish and then present your baits there. Location of fish is then automatic: if there is natural food, there will be some form of visual feeding activity at some time of the day or night. If you go about locating your quarry by locating their feeding areas you cannot fail, unlesss you are doing something else wrong!

4 Tackle

So much has happened in recent years with carp fishing tackle that even the new ideas and methods discussed and illustrated in this book may well be out of fashion by the time of publication and replaced by more methods to confuse even the most active and experienced carp anglers. The following will be an introduction to some basics and also some sophistications in tackle items. There may not be a need for full sophistication in tackle to start with, but it would be wise to consider buying the best you can afford, particularly with rods, reels and monofilament line. There is so much variety in some items that it is impossible to examine everything in the space available; many items get tested in the monthly and weekly publications by good anglers and it would be worthwhile looking to these for up-to-date appraisals!

RODS

Walk into any good tackle dealer or pick up any angling publication weekly or monthly and you will usually find displayed a vast array of rods and blanks to suit any application; from short range to extreme range, light lines to heavy lines, the choice will be yours. Development in rods has led to some configurations in design to cater for all types of water, from vast oceans of gravel pits to small secluded pools. There are compound-action rods for light-line, close-range work, fast taper rods for extreme range

and, more recently, rods designed with a wide band of application to cover short-range, mid-range and long-range fishing. These multi-range rods are proving very useful for anglers who tend to fish in a number of different types of water and maybe at varying ranges on one water. It might be a good investment for the newcomer to investigate the possibility of using one of these rods, for the initial period, until some basic understanding is obtained. Disappointment is in one way or another guaranteed if you choose either too light an action, or too heavy an action, without matching them to the job in hand, so do think carefully!

Listed in Table 1 opposite you will see a good selection of rod blanks and finished rods. The ones recommended are proven and reliable. Some fibreglass rods and blanks are available, but with the current cost of carbon fibre blanks and rods being what they are, it would be wise to purchase either in carbon. Cheap carbon rods are not recommended; you get what you pay for, so buy the best you can afford! A new material that has now become widely used by many manufacturers is Kevlar fibre and if you can, again, afford it, purchase either blanks or rods using this material.

Rods have grown in length since Richard Walker's MK IV carp rods of ten feet; eleven foot was the next length in fibreglass rods, and today we have rods available from eleven to thirteen feet, so you would be wise to consider a twelve-foot rod as your ideal! Test curves vary from 1¼ pounds to 2¾ pounds. Multi-range rods tend to be around 2

Make	Material	Test Curve	Lines	Length	Action
1. North Western	Carbon/Kevlar	2lb	6–12lb	12ft	Compound
2. North Western	Carbon/Kevlar	2½lb	8–15lb	12ft	M/Fast taper
3. Diawa	Whisker/Carbon Kevlar	1½lb	6–10lb	12ft	Compound
4. Diawa	Whisker/Carbon Kevlar	2½lb	8–15lb	12ft	M/Fast taper
5. Tricast ER	Diamond Kevlar/Carbon	2½lb fast	8–15lb	12ft	Fast taper
6. Tricast Mur	Carbon/Kevlar	2lb	6–13lb	12ft	Compound
7. Tricast M-L	Carbon/Kevlar	2¼lb	7–14lb	12ft	M/Fast taper
8. North Western	Fibreglass/SS5	2lb	8–15lb	11ft	Compound
9. North Western	Fibreglass/SS6	2¼lb	8–15lb	11ft	Fast taper

Table 1 Rods and blanks

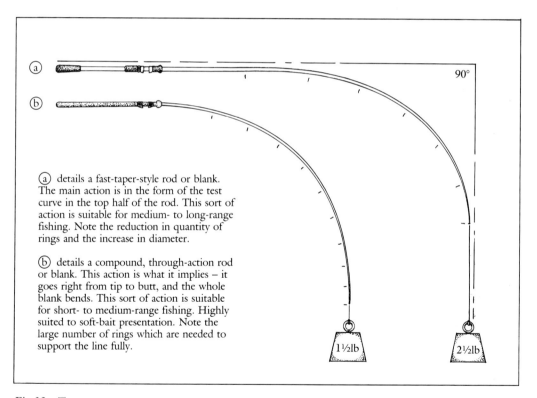

ⓐ details a fast-taper-style rod or blank. The main action is in the form of the test curve in the top half of the rod. This sort of action is suitable for medium- to long-range fishing. Note the reduction in quantity of rings and the increase in diameter.

ⓑ details a compound, through-action rod or blank. This action is what it implies – it goes right from tip to butt, and the whole blank bends. This sort of action is suitable for short- to medium-range fishing. Highly suited to soft-bait presentation. Note the large number of rings which are needed to support the line fully.

Fig 13 Test curves

pounds' test curve and this will allow you to use monofilament lines from 9 to 15 pounds' breaking strain. The action of these rods is a compound, through action which allows them to bend at their full test curve from tip to butt, similar to that shown in Fig 13. The thing to remember with rod choice is balance; you should choose a complete outfit of rod, reel and line to suit the type of carp fishing you will spend most of your time actually doing.

REELS

Development in fixed spool reels has not stood still; manufacturers have taken heed of the size of the specialist fishing market and have provided anglers with what they have been asking for: smoother drag systems (clutches), higher gear ratios, large-capacity spools, lightness, and specialised line control in the form of free spooling, only available previously on multiplier reels. Good-quality reels are a must to match the rod and the monofilament lines you will use, be they light for casting long distances or heavy for snag fishing.

Many types and makes are now available to meet any need, but remember you will get what you pay for; if you want durability and

reliability then pay as much as you can and buy a proven reel, possibly from one listed below in Table 2.

The most recent innovation in reel design is the specialised free-spool mode, built into reels like the Shimano 'Baitrunner' series, Mitchell 3350RD and Abu Garcia 654GT. These allow for minimum drag to be employed for 'closed bail arm' fishing; a simple turn of the handle on the Shimano and Abu models switches the drag into a preselect tension, while on the 3350RD a special drag lever can be pulled with the middle finger when the rod is picked up which allows the drag to be tightened to suit the situation. The rear drag can then be adjusted to a midway point to allow the fish to be played on a lighter setting without the need for finger action. Should you require to apply more pressure or deal with surging run you can apply or release the 'fighting drag lever' as required. Other models in the Shimano range are now coming onto the market with similar ideas. You should take a close look at these reels at your nearest stockist to see how they might suit your type of carp fishing.

Where your need is to equip yourself with quality, minus gimmicks, you would be well advised to consider other models in the Abu, Shimano and Mitchell ranges. Purchase a reel like the Mitchell 300S skirted spool reel, or

| Make | Model | Line Capacity | | | Ratio |
		8lb	10lb	12lb	
1. Mitchell	300S/301S	380yd	330yd	300yd	
2. Mitchell	225ORD	330yd	240yd	200yd	
3. Mitchell	335ORD/FC	305yd	240yd	200yd	
4. Shimano	TSS3500	305yd	–	230yd	4.6:1
5. Shimano	BTR3500	305yd	–	230yd	4.6:1
6. Abu Garcia	Cardinal 654GT	250yd	200yd	–	

Table 2   Reels

the Mitchell 2250RD rear drag model which can be used with clutch backed off, but it is more cumbersome and *not* advised for closed bail fishing with the anti-reverse 'on'.

LINES

To make the tackle balance correctly, the choice of line is a very important factor. After all, it is the means of connecting you with your quarry, and if you get the balance wrong you risk breakage on the cast, the strike or during the fight to land your fish. The type and strength of line you choose should be related to the style of fishing and to the tackle you will use. Many makes and types of line exist, some of which have a high degree of stretch, while others are of low stretch; both have their applications and should be used accordingly. Your main requirement for ninety per cent of your carp fishing will be served by the normal high-stretch line. Typical examples are Maxima Chameleon and Sylcast Sorrel; both have a sound pedigree and are used by a large proportion of today's carp anglers. The breaking strain you would be well advised to use would be 9 pounds in Sylcast or 10 pounds in Maxima for normal conditions, and up to 15 pounds in both

brands for snaggy waters where the line might rub on abrasive surfaces like branches, gravel bars, zebra mussels, etc. The strength of your line must balance with your rod's test curve, so whilst you are recommended to use the strongest line, remember that this will depend on the rod you choose to use. With our guideline of 2- to 2½-pound test curve medium-action rods, a 9- to 15-pound breaking-strain line can be safely used – remember that this balance is going to be needed to allow you to cast safely anything up to two ounces of lead smoothly without breakage of line or rod. Table 3 shows a list of lines and their particular characteristics and uses. Fig 14 shows a correctly filled spool.

KNOTS

An important point to remember with nylon monofilament line is that it is only as strong as the weakest point which is usually the knot. To ensure you get the best knot strength, a useful and practical variety of knots appear in Figs 15, 16, 17 and 18. Great care should be taken when tying your knots, and all of them should be moistened to make them slide smoothly to the tightened position. Do not rush the tightening; take

Make	Strength/BS	Diameter
1. Sylcast Sorrel	7lb/3.0kg	0.10in/2.5mm
2. Sylcast Sorrel	9lb/4.0kg	0.12in/3.0mm
3. Sylcast Sorrel	11lb/5.0kg	0.13in/3.2mm
4. Maxima Chameleon	8lb/3.6kg	0.10in/2.5mm
5. Maxima Chameleon	10lb/4.5kg	0.12in/3.0mm
6. Maxima Chameleon	12lb/5.5kg	0.13in/3.2mm
7. Drennan Specimen Plus	8lb/3.6kg	0.11in/2.7mm
8. Drennan Specimen Plus	10lb/4.5kg	0.12in/3.0mm

Table 3   Lines

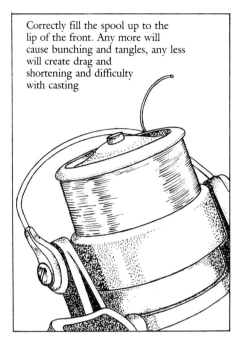

Correctly fill the spool up to the lip of the front. Any more will cause bunching and tangles, any less will create drag and shortening and difficulty with casting

Fig 14   Correctly filled spool

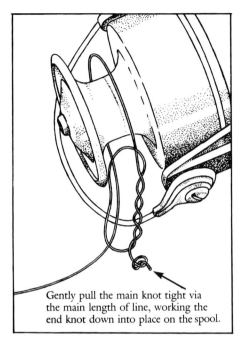

Gently pull the main knot tight via the main length of line, working the end knot down into place on the spool.

Fig 15   Knot for attaching line to spool

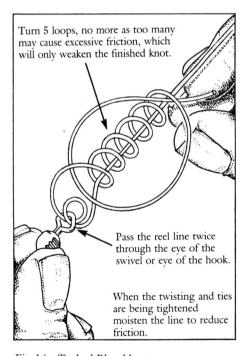

Turn 5 loops, no more as too many may cause excessive friction, which will only weaken the finished knot.

Pass the reel line twice through the eye of the swivel or eye of the hook.

When the twisting and ties are being tightened moisten the line to reduce friction.

Fig 16   Tucked Blood knot

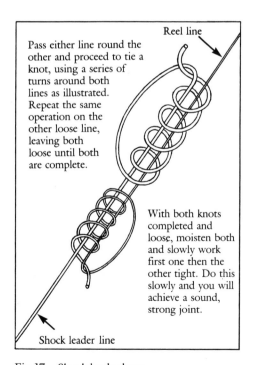

Reel line

Pass either line round the other and proceed to tie a knot, using a series of turns around both lines as illustrated. Repeat the same operation on the other loose line, leaving both loose until both are complete.

With both knots completed and loose, moisten both and slowly work first one then the other tight. Do this slowly and you will achieve a sound, strong joint.

Shock leader line

Fig 17   Shock leader knot

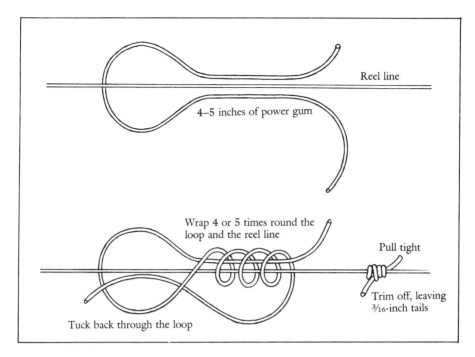

Reel line

4–5 inches of power gum

Wrap 4 or 5 times round the loop and the reel line

Pull tight

Trim off, leaving
³/₁₆-inch tails

Tuck back through the loop

Fig 18   Stop knot (power gum)

time and you will get a stronger finish. Remember, it could make the difference between landing and losing that big carp!

TERMINAL TACKLE

Moving from line and on to terminal tackle such as hooks, swivels, hook links and weights, this forms possibly the most important part of tackle. It is through these items that you will or will not achieve correct bait presentation and the optimum chance to hook the fish which is fooled into taking your bait. The ability to balance finely the terminal tackle with the other tackle and to match this to the circumstances of the swim being fished will hopefully result in a carp on the bank! Fig 19 illustrates three of the various types of swivel available. Probably the most useful is the 'Diamond-Eye' swivel obtainable from Drennan Tackle or Kevin Nash Tackle. With

this style of swivel the reel line and hooklink (of nylon or dacron, etc.) will sit neatly in the centre of the eye. Also illustrated are some of the clip links that can be used with these swivels. Probably of most service will be the Drennan 'Safeloc' in the centre which can benefit by being covered in a short length of silicon rubber to prevent snagging of line during the cast. To these links you will probably attach the suitable size of leger weights, but remember that you must use non-toxic material bombs for weights up to 2 ounces. There are various types and shapes of bomb, designed for casting distances or for making into anti-tangle rigs. Illustrated in Fig 20 are some of the various bombs available.

From the reel-line swivel to the hook you may choose to use either monofilament line or alternatively dacron, braided nylon or dental floss, waxed or plain. The choice of these will be yours but you would be well advised to try each in an attempt to find the one type suitable

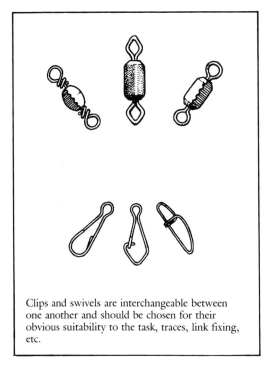

Clips and swivels are interchangeable between one another and should be chosen for their obvious suitability to the task, traces, link fixing, etc.

Fig 19   Swivel assortment with clips

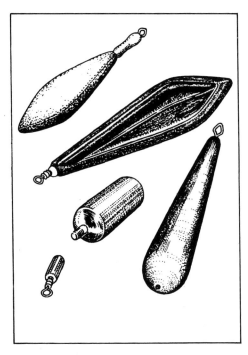

Fig 20   Assortment of lead and non-toxic leger weights

Make	Material	Colour	BS
Masterbraid	Dacron	White	6lb, 10lb, 12lb
Sylcast	Dacron	Black	6lb, 10lb, 12lb
Berkeley	Braided nylon	Camouflaged	Multiple strands of fine nylon
	Waxed dental floss	White	Approx. 12lb
	Unwaxed dental floss	Natural	Approx. 12lb
Kryston	Multi-strand material	Natural	230 continuous strands of fibre–70lb

Table 4   Hooklink materials

to the water being fished – on some waters the carp have become educated to avoid certain materials! Choice of brands and breaking strain will depend on availability. Table 4 details some makes of hooklink material and their respective breaking strains and other characteristics. The braided types of hooklink require a more specialised knot than a Tucked Blood knot which might slip and unravel. To ensure not only full security from slipping but, if properly tied and tightened, a very strong and reliable hold use the Palomar knot. The method of tying it is illustrated in Figs 21 and 22.

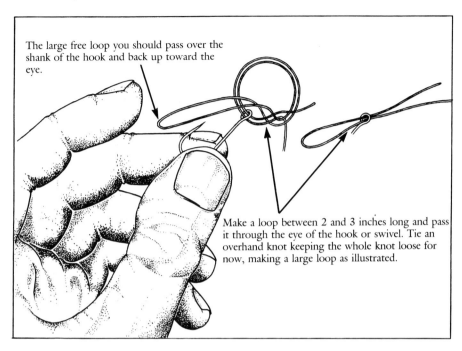

The large free loop you should pass over the shank of the hook and back up toward the eye.

Make a loop between 2 and 3 inches long and pass it through the eye of the hook or swivel. Tie an overhand knot keeping the whole knot loose for now, making a large loop as illustrated.

Fig 21   Palomar knot for dacron, etc.

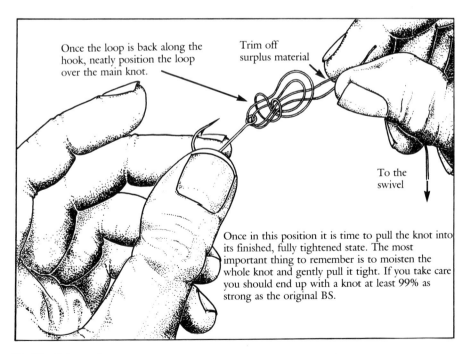

Once the loop is back along the hook, neatly position the loop over the main knot.

Trim off surplus material

To the swivel

Once in this position it is time to pull the knot into its finished, fully tightened state. The most important thing to remember is to moisten the whole knot and gently pull it tight. If you take care you should end up with a knot at least 99% as strong as the original BS.

Fig 22   Palomar knot

HOOKS

The hook is another item of tackle that has
seen dramatic levels of development in the
last couple of years. The original special carp
hook was the modified, solder-blob, low-
water salmon hook. Since then numerous
designs of hook have appeared in a ready-to-
use form from many of the hook manufacturers. Listed in Table 5 are a number of good
quality hooks that have been found to be
reliable in both strength and hooking
capability.

Many of the hooks available today are
supplied with a chemically etched point,
making them sharper than you could ever
expect to get with sharpening stones. If you
choose a pattern of hook that is not supplied
in this form it is advisable to hone the point
as sharply as you can with a suitable hook
sharpening stone! It may even be necessary to
re-sharpen the hook during use, particularly
after the capture of a fish or after several re-
casts if you are fishing on gravel bars, etc.
Even if you are using chemically sharpened
hooks, make a point of checking the
condition of your hook for these reasons.

Presentation style will dictate which hook
you should use. Wide-gape, round-bend type
hooks will be necessary for hook-mounted
baits, shank or eye for paste baits and bread

in its various forms. Slightly larger sizes, like
sizes 4 or 2, will probably be required as well.
These will ensure the point is clear to find a
hold when most of the hook is obscured by
the bait.

Off-hook tactics with the various hair
options used with boiled bottom baits and
floaters, etc., succeed with smaller hook sizes
from maybe size 4 down to size 8; with the
smaller baits these sizes will be needed to
counter presentation difficulties on hard-
fished waters. The same tactics have been the
background to development of specialist
patterns of hook to aid hook holds and
penetration. Confidence will be gained in
using one style of hook, so try as many as
possible and see which suits your style or
methods. Remember to vary the hook to suit
each method of presentation and always be
sure to fish with the sharpest possible hook.

BAIT MOUNTING

To mount your baits, particles, boilies or
floaters on hairs, stringers, etc., you will need
a variety of needles, as shown in Fig 24, a
spool of very light nylon monofilament or
thread to mount baits on, and some PVA
string to secure the baits to casting booms
and mounting stringers, etc.

Name	Model	Sizes Recommended
Kevin Nash	Hair-rig Hook	
Kevin Nash	Super Specialist Carp Hook	
Rod Hutchinson	Special Extra Strong Carp Hook	
Partridge	21 Jack Hilton Carp Hook	8–2
Partridge	211 Kevin Maddock's Hair-Rig Hook	
Drennan	Super Specialist Hook	
Simpson of Turnford	Carp Catcher Hook	

Table 5   Hooks

Dean Allen responds to his indicators moving on a club carp lake.

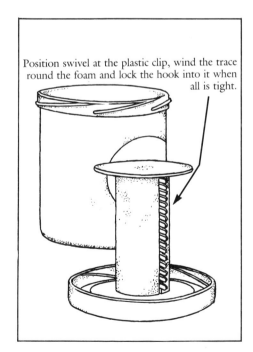

Position swivel at the plastic clip, wind the trace round the foam and lock the hook into it when all is tight.

Fig 23   Trace tidy

The final items of tackle you will require are bite indicators. The best is the Optonic (*see* Fig 28), its roller system being the most sensitive in recording drop-back, slack-line bites and conventional full-blooded runs and twitchy takes! The indicator you choose to use will depend on your budget. There are some economically priced Antenna-type buzzers available which will give the same results in indicating full-blooded runs and twitchy takes, but not drop-back-type bites. With some methods, particularly semi-fixed leads, these are very common, so choose well or save up for an Optonic-style indicator!

While waiting to buy, you would be advised to purchase some of the rod rest heads shown in Fig 27. These are essential for the free passage of line when used with the monkey-climber-style indicator or the plastic tube indicators, shown in Fig 26. These will give good visual indication of both full takes, etc., and drop-back if they occur. Not every

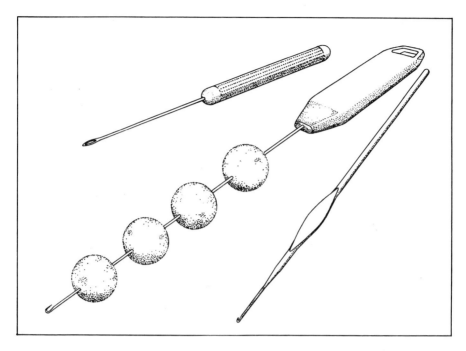

Fig 24   Baiting and stringer needles

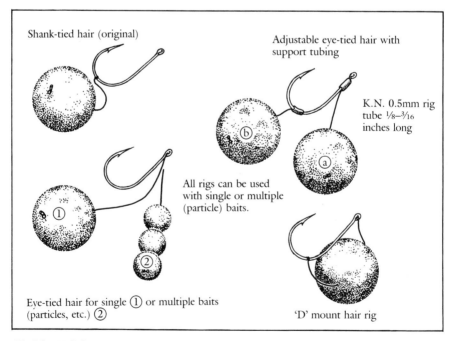

Shank-tied hair (original)

Adjustable eye-tied hair with
support tubing

ⓑ

K.N. 0.5mm rig
tube ⅛–³⁄₁₆
inches long

ⓐ

①

All rigs can be used
with single or multiple
(particle) baits.

②

Eye-tied hair for single ① or multiple baits
(particles, etc.) ②

'D' mount hair rig

Fig 25   Hair layouts

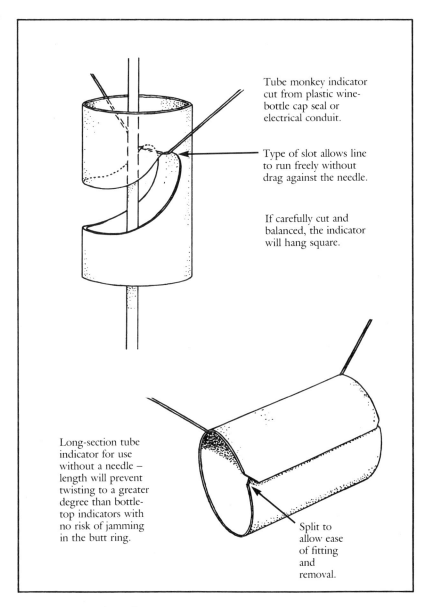

Tube monkey indicator
cut from plastic wine-
bottle cap seal or
electrical conduit.

Type of slot allows line
to run freely without
drag against the needle.

If carefully cut and
balanced, the indicator
will hang square.

Long-section tube
indicator for use
without a needle –
length will prevent
twisting to a greater
degree than bottle-
top indicators with
no risk of jamming
in the butt ring.

Split to
allow ease
of fitting
and
removal.

Fig 26   Plastic bite indicators

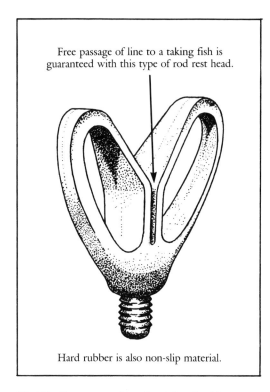

Free passage of line to a taking fish is guaranteed with this type of rod rest head.

Hard rubber is also non-slip material.

Fig 27   Drennan rod rest head (hard rubber)

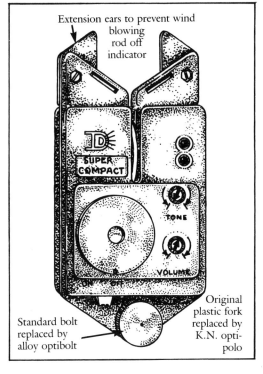

Extension ears to prevent wind blowing rod off indicator

SUPER COMPACT

TONE

VOLUME

ON OFF

Standard bolt replaced by alloy optibolt

Original plastic fork replaced by K.N. opti-polo

Fig 28   Optonic indicator (Super)

session calls for the use of audible indicators, so do not worry if you cannot afford them – use the ordinary rod rest to start with and stay with your rods! Other bite indicators to carry will be a small selection of floats for margin fishing, etc., and some surface bait controllers in various weights to allow good presentation close to and away from the bank.

There are many other items of tackle you can accumulate and carry, and we all end up carrying our own ideal selection. The essentials are covered here and if you follow these basic guidelines and the suggestions made in the various other chapters you will be in a sound position to succeed in your task.

5 Baits

Walk into any good tackle dealer's and you will find some part of the display dedicated to carp baits, either ready-made baits or the ingredients to make any recipe you could imagine. Many changes have taken place since Richard Walker's record forty-four pound fish was taken on balanced crust!

Today's carp angler has at his fingertips endless varieties of recipes for specials, pastes, boilies, particles, floaters, etc. Many are now packaged, ready-cooked and prepared for instant use, making it very easy to get amongst the carp on any of the carp waters throughout the country. The majority of these packaged baits are extremely effective, being based upon proven recipes established by talented carp anglers over many seasons – at least that is what the advertisements inform us!

That some of the commercial baits are outstanding is beyond question, though some recipes do not live up to the reputation and are more difficult to tempt fish on. The good ones do have advantages in that they allow you to fish confidently knowing the bait *does* attract and catch fish, thus allowing you to concentrate on getting presentation right or any of the other problems that may eat into your confidence if the bites start to slow up or stop. However, after you have gone through all the presentation, location, climatic and pressure solving procedures to catch more carp, you could well end up scratching your head, not knowing why you cannot catch any more carp.

The one question that you may have failed to answer fully is whether the bait could be to blame. Suddenly you catch on: the fish have become wary of the colour, the flavour or the texture, or all three, due to the amount of fish caught on the same bait, and if you are smart you will move on to a new bait. Whether you try another commercial bait or change to one of your own making depends on how much experience you have of making baits. If you got into carp fishing with ready-made baits you will not have gained any back-up experience of testing home-made baits by trial and error.

The problem of not catching fish can lead to a preoccupation with trial and error which in itself can be self-defeating, and can prevent you gaining experience that is positive. You must avoid quick changes in bait recipe, flavouring and colouring combinations. Many of the mixes do not catch instantly and if you immediately move on to another and so on, you might never succeed with any of them.

The other extreme is when you come up with a new bait and catch instantly. Then, convinced that you have come up with the wonder bait, you set up to use the bait blindly and after several sessions of not catching you become convinced it is the rig that is to blame. So you experiment with that blindly, fishing confidently with the bait which could be blown or even repellent to your quarry.

To come to terms with the subject of baits and how to use them, go back to basics and consider what baits exist, slowly working through them and identifying what they have

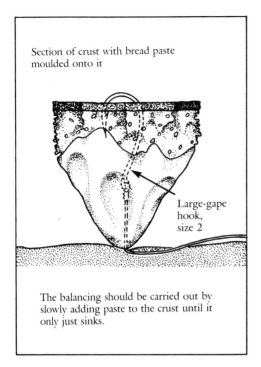

Section of crust with bread paste moulded onto it

Large-gape hook, size 2

The balancing should be carried out by slowly adding paste to the crust until it only just sinks.

Fig 29   Balanced crust

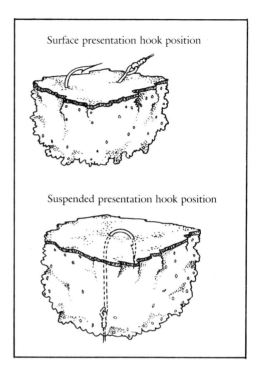

Surface presentation hook position

Suspended presentation hook position

Fig 30   Hooking crust

been useful, why they have been successful and maybe why they can be successful again. Many of the very old types and styles of bait will still catch and have never in fact stopped catching carp, big and small. Many of the fish in a great number of carp fisheries will never have seen some of the old-style baits like basic flavoured bread paste, sausage meat, luncheon meat, etc. They fell out of fashion long before many of today's fish were stocked!

The best way to show which sorts of bait can be used to attract and catch carp from the many different types of carp fishery that exist and how they should be used is to categorise the various baits and then detail how and why to make and use them.

BREAD BAITS

Bread forms one of the basic baits and is the first bait many of us use for all species. When considering what makes up bread it is possible that we could classify it as the original special bait, but because it is so readily available in so many different forms we tend to take it for granted. Think about the flour and yeast and how they are processed and mixed and then think back to how both ingredients were cultivated and specifically grown, rather like some of today's ingredients as used in today's specials! The baking of bread varies from recipe to recipe and with this comes different textures of flake and crust, suitable for many presentation requirements. There is more to bread and its use as a bait than immediately meets the eye!

Richard Walker's idea of balanced crust was probably the first identified way to attract big carp and Fig 29 shows how to prepare this effective way of presenting bread, particularly in weedy swims where dense baits may get concealed in thick soft weed beds or blanket weed. The general way to present this has entailed free-lining at close range. It can also be used with leger tactics fished in conjunction with a long tail from weight to hook, but preferably it is a close-range, weight-free technique.

Bread crust alone, with a good portion of flake, allows surface presentation in gaps on weed beds, by lily pads or in open water. It also allows sunken presentation, high in the water, midway or just off the bottom as illustrated in Fig 31. One disadvantage of bread crust on the surface is the visual attraction for water fowl and seagulls – they spot it from miles away! Flavourings and

colourings can be added to bread, particularly if you decide to bake your own from some of the mixes available in grocery stores today. This can then be made up into all forms of bread bait. Waterfowl and gulls seem to take less interest in green, brown, or any other suitably dull-coloured surface baits and this also applies to bread, so it is worth giving coloured crust a try.

Bread flake is probably the most underused but most abused of bread bait presentations, and perhaps the latter is the reason for the former situation! Yet so many big fish of all species fall to the simple bait of bread flake, and carp are no exception. The key to success with flake lies in how it is presented, whether it is on the surface, at mid-depth, on the drop, on the bottom, or on the weed. Fig 32 illustrates some presentations of bread flake.

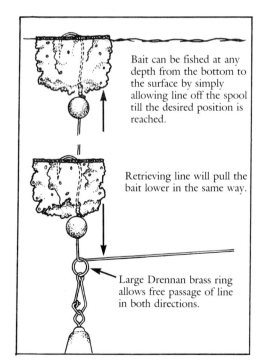

Bait can be fished at any depth from the bottom to the surface by simply allowing line off the spool till the desired position is reached.

Retrieving line will pull the bait lower in the same way.

Large Drennan brass ring allows free passage of line in both directions.

Fig 31   Suspended crust

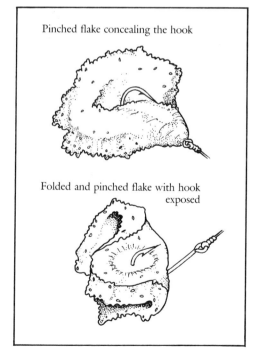

Pinched flake concealing the hook

Folded and pinched flake with hook exposed

Fig 32   Pinched and folded bread flake

A mid-double mirror carp taken on bread flake from a Nature Reserve fishery.

Whichever presentation you aim for, the one key factor in presentation is the quality and texture of the flake you use on the hook.

To obtain the best possible texture from either the flake or crust, choose a freshly baked loaf and one with a close texture which is moist but not stodgy; the one that is commonly called a sandwich loaf fits perfectly. Too dry or openly textured bread is difficult to use because it will not mould properly on the hook and if you do achieve a reasonable finish the hook is more than likely to be obscured. Too stodgy a loaf and you will not get the correct action and probably not get a surface bait to float. A good moist, smooth-textured bread will require only a light pinch to attach it neatly to the hook (*see* Fig 32), and the size can be varied along with the degree of pinching to achieve a floating bait, a slow floating and sinking action or a bait that settles gently on weed or silt. Once in the water the bread flake will swell slightly and soften to allow the hook to come free readily on the strike. If the bait stays on the hook after retrieving the cast it is not right, so change to a different bread mix or lighten up on the pinching.

At the beginning of this chapter, reference was made to Richard Walker's method of using balanced crust to capture his big carp. For this, the combination of crust and flake, or crust and bread paste is used to achieve a balance of such a fine degree that the bait, when mounted on the hook, only just sinks. This will allow it to settle gently on silt, weed or gravel as with flake, but more importantly it will remain intact and also buoyant for longer, and will be able to react to the sucking action of the carp more effectively, not coming off the hook! Fig 29 shows the make-up of a balanced crust bait.

Bread paste is the one bait that requires greatest care in getting it right. There are two ways of making a paste bait from bread and these require the use of stale sliced or unsliced bread and sliced fresh bread respectively. Flavouring the paste can make it more attractive and this can be achieved by adding any suitable ingredient you wish during the mixing. Typical ingredients are honey, flavourings and sweeteners, cheese, fish and meat pastes, etc.; colourings can even be added to enhance or subdue the visual aspect of the bait.

Simple bread paste is best made with stale bread, since this has a texture which crumbles easily in the palms of your hands, and a small amount of liquid ingredients and colouring can be added to form a smooth paste. At first it will probably be a bit wet but this can be stiffened by slowly adding more crumbled bread and a little plain flour. When mixed, keep folding and kneading the doughy paste until it is moist and smooth.

The method of making paste with fresh bread is done with a sliced loaf, either medium or thick sliced. Lay out the slices, cut off all the crusts and spread the additional soft and creamy ingredients liberally over each slice. Then put one slice on top of another and, with four or five slices at a time, mould and knead them until they are all blended together. If the mixture is too stiff add a little water or more additive to moisten further, then continue kneading into a smooth paste.

With both methods keep working the bait until smooth and soft. It can then be moulded onto the hook with the point showing. Some mixes using cheese may stiffen in cool water so they should be mixed a little softer to allow for this. Fig 33 shows the paste moulded onto the hook. In most circumstances all the bread baits will withstand casting but you will probably find that some are best fished on a free-line basis and therefore are restricted to short-range fishing. Other methods will also be seen in later chapters.

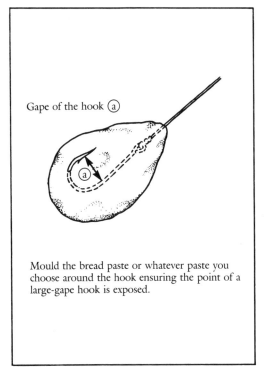

Gape of the hook (a)

(a)

Mould the bread paste or whatever paste you choose around the hook ensuring the point of a large-gape hook is exposed.

Hook the whole worm through the strongest point. The white collar band allows a good hold and ensures the worm remains active for a reasonable amount of time.

Fig 33   Bread paste on the hook

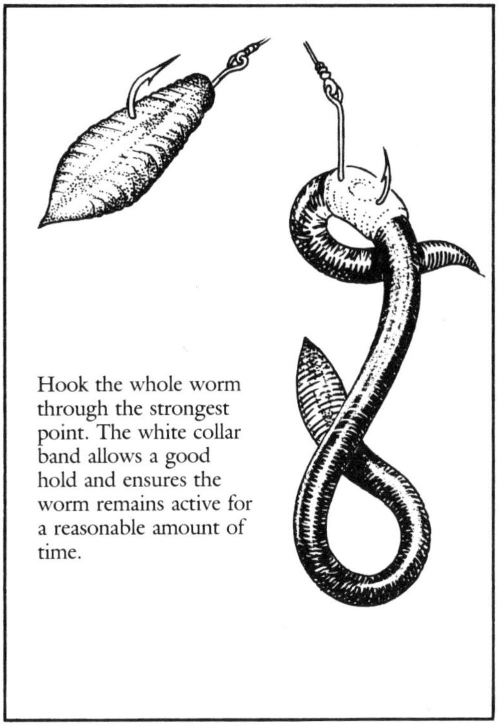

Fig 34   Lobworm, whole

NATURAL AND LIVE BAITS

The only really good worm is a lively one, although half and tail sections do catch carp (*see* Fig 34). Lobworms, redworms, brandlings, maggots, etc., make handy baits when trying to tempt wary feeding carp which may be seen at close range. They are also useful when carp are feeding in silty areas, for if the bait is out of sight the vibration of the worm wriggling will be felt by the probing, sensitive barbules on the carp's snout. Fig 35 shows how to attach worms to the hook and Fig 36 shows their presentation. A supply of worms is worthwhile if you are fishing small waters where the carp can be seen feeding close in. Present them with a worm or worms on lightly weighted float tackle for exciting sport.

Having covered the old standard baits of bread and worms, it is worth remembering that very few people will be using them on most waters. So when things are slow and bites hard to come by or maybe just for a change, try using some of these old *simple* methods – the carp may never have seen any of them! The same can be said of the next baits we will discuss.

CONVENIENCE BAITS

Convenience baits are those requiring little or no mixing or preparation. In this category we can include the very successful ones: sausage, luncheon meat, sweetcorn. Cooked sausage and luncheon meat can be sliced and cubed

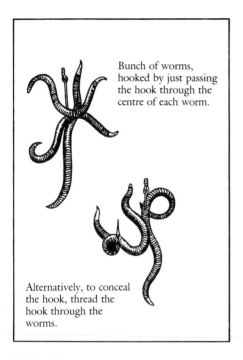

Bunch of worms, hooked by just passing the hook through the centre of each worm.

Alternatively, to conceal the hook, thread the hook through the worms.

Fig 35   Brandlings or redworms on the hook

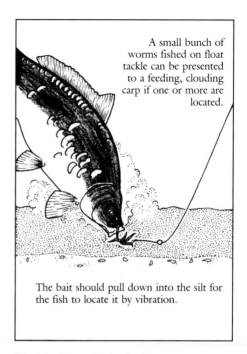

A small bunch of worms fished on float tackle can be presented to a feeding, clouding carp if one or more are located.

The bait should pull down into the silt for the fish to locate it by vibration.

Fig 36   Worm fishing in silt

Dice the luncheon meat into cubes of ⅜- to ½-inch square and either mount them directly onto the hook ① or onto a shank-tied hair.②

Fig 37   Luncheon meat

to any size, large or small, to provide an attractive bait (*see* Fig 37) which on even the hardest water can prove the downfall of very big carp, though they have gone out of fashion with anglers. Sweetcorn has been extremely successful, being very visible and of a very attractive taste. But this has had its shortcomings in that convenience and availability can lead to carp becoming extremely wary of piles of sweet-tasting, yellow sweetcorn, as many anglers use it as bait. Two answers should cure this problem: change the colour or change the flavour of the bait, or ultimately change both. The way to effect this is by adding five millilitres of flavouring and sweetener, mixed together, to a large tin of sweetcorn. To colour your bait, add a small quantity of colouring at a time until you achieve the strength of colour you wish. Even when you are adding only colour to your bait, add a couple of millilitres of sweetener to take the edge off the bitter taste of the colouring,

The golden glow of an autumn day and a common carp of 11lb.

which might taint the bait. Some colour and flavour combinations worth a try are red and strawberry, and brown and maple.

Sweetcorn falls into the category of particle fishing and many other baits fall into this category. Particles can be any small bait which is fished in quantity; under this heading come the various varieties of peas, beans, nuts, seeds and any large bait diced or rolled to a small size.

There are too many different kinds of particle bait to list every one, but some of the most successful are maple peas, chick peas, blackeye beans, peanuts and tiger nuts. All are dry in their original state and, unlike sweetcorn, require soaking and cooking prior to use. Some tinned varieties of particles are available in supermarkets, such as red kidney beans, chick peas, cannellini beans, etc., which do offer a handy alternative. The only drawback is that they are usually cooked to a very soft state, making hooking a little difficult!

Particle Baits

Hemp	Cashew nuts
Tares	Haricot beans
Blackeye beans	Butter beans
Maple peas	Sunflower seeds
Chick peas	Dun peas
Peanuts	Buckwheat
Tiger nuts	Pumpkin seeds

Soak for twenty-four hours. Add flavourings and sweeteners, etc., to the water when soaking. Cook in the same water until soft enough for hooking. Test bait during cooking to assess condition and note the time taken for future reference.

As these bait items are all stored dry they will absorb water and subsequently swell to at least twice the dried size. To allow for this,

when preparing any of the mentioned baits, including peanuts and tiger nuts, add twice as much water to the container as you put in of bait. For example, add two pints (1 litre) of water with two millilitres of salt to one pint (0.5 litre) of bait and soak for at least twenty-four hours, adding water as necessary to keep the bait completely covered. If you intend to flavour your bait, it is best to add this to the water at the beginning of the soak. With one pint (0.5 litre) of bait add ten millilitres of flavouring and maybe ten millilitres of sweetener if you want a sweet flavour; add five millilitres of salt for a savoury flavour. Once soaking is completed you should place the bait and flavoured water into a saucepan or pressure cooker and cook until the bait is soft enough for hooking. The cooking also has the effect of neutralising harmful chemicals in some of the pea and bean varieties, notably red kidney beans.

With the nuts, cooking will break down and release their natural oils so making for a natural attractor in conjunction with any added flavourings. It can be useful to add salt or sweetener to match the type of flavouring, and it can pay to try a sweet savoury mixture, particularly if everyone else is sticking to traditional flavourings. Fig 38 shows how to employ particle baits to their best advantage, depending on just how and where you intend to use them. This is covered in more detail in Chapter 7 (see page 106).

HIGH PROTEIN AND HIGH NUTRITIONAL VALUE BAITS

This brings us to the more complex and probably the more selective types of bait. The need for these arose with the increased interest in carp fishing and the greater number of fish which were becoming wary of the regular baits. The first and probably the

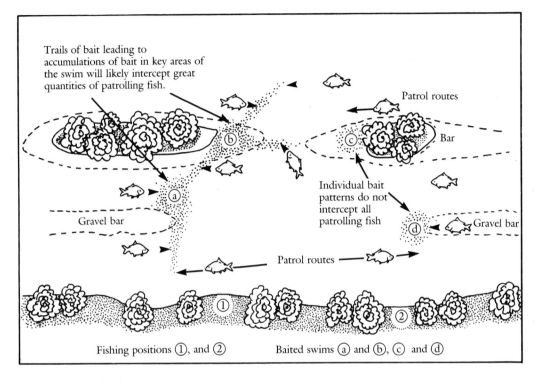

Trails of bait leading to accumulations of bait in key areas of the swim will likely intercept great quantities of patrolling fish.

Patrol routes

Bar

Individual bait patterns do not intercept all patrolling fish

Gravel bar

Gravel bar

Patrol routes

Fishing positions ① and ②   Baited swims ⓐ and ⓑ, ⓒ and ⓓ

Fig 38   How to bait with particles

most inventive angler to exploit the HNV (High Nutritional Value) theory was Fred Wilton. Basically, this was an extension of mixes of different items into a paste-type bait similar to the bread paste with cheese, fish or meat paste mixes. The main difference was in the way individual ingredients were isolated from certain food items, particularly from milk. Many of the ingredients are of high protein value which enables a combination of these to be used together or individually added to a particular food source to enhance its value, as has been employed with our own foods and animal feeds for many years. Here is a list of useful ingredients which can be added to or used to make up either HNV or enhanced (high protein) paste baits.

Lactic casein (various grades available)
Sodium caseinate
Calcium caseinate (Casilan)
Lactalbumin
Egg albumen
Soya isolate
Soya flour
Wheat gluten
Equivite (milk pellets)
Pruteen

PYM (Philips Yeast Mixture)
Brewers yeast (Healthilife, etc.)
Shrimp meal
White fish meal
Meat and bone meal
Molasses meal
Peanut meal
Robin red
Trout pellets

High protein baits and high nutritional value baits are similar in principle but require a different approach in the way they are used. High protein pastes will usually contain what their names imply, a high concentration of high protein ingredients in a suitable binder which will allow a practical bait to be made. When combined with a suitable flavouring these pastes will attract carp and encourage them to pick up the bait, which they will find palatable very quickly. Two good HP bait recipes are given below.

(1) *7oz (200g) casein*
    1oz (28g)
    Equivite
    (pellets)
    1oz (28g) egg
    albumen
    1oz (28g) calcium
    caseinate

(2) *5oz (140g) casein*
    2oz (56g)
    Equivite
    (pellets)
    1oz (28g)
    lactalbumin
    1oz (28g) soya
    flour
    1oz (28g) calcium
    caseinate

Mix with 6 eggs (max.) or approx. 150ml water, adding colouring, 5ml of flavouring and 5ml of sweetener to the eggs prior to the dry ingredients. Introduce dry ingredients slowly to the eggs, mixing and adding in stages. Mix to a firm paste and allow to stand five to ten minutes. Roll into balls. Use within twenty-four hours or freeze and use within twenty-four hours after defrosting.

The HNV baits are an extension of HP baits and form the majority of baits produced today. Their purpose is to supply, as Fred Wilton's theory suggested, as much of the carps' dietary requirement as possible to the extent that if sufficient bait is fed to the fish over an extended period they will identify the food source as one satisfying their bodily needs. Eventually they should seek out and eat the bait without fear and almost to the exclusion of their usual food. Many large catches of fish to individual anglers have shown that this does in fact occur.

A good HNV bait will not be made out of high protein ingredients alone but a combination of proteins, minerals, carbohydrates, vitamins, fats and oils in a carefully balanced form. A selection of proven HNV recipes follows which use some of the HNV ingredients listed on page 56.

(1) *3oz (85g) casein*
    1oz (28g)
    lactalbumin
    1oz (28g)
    Equivite
    (pellets)
    2oz (56g) yeast
    (Healthilife)
    1oz (28g)
    wheatgerm
    1oz (28g) gluten

(2) *3oz (85g) casein*
    1oz (28g)
    lactalbumin
    1oz (28g)
    Equivite
    (pellets)
    2oz (56g)
    wheatgerm
    1oz (28g) gluten
    1oz (28g)
    calcium
    caseinate
    1oz soya flour/
    isolate

(3) *4oz (110g) casein*
    1oz (28g)
    lactalbumin
    1oz (28g)
    Equivite
    (pellets)
    2oz (56g)
    wheatgerm
    1oz (28g) gluten
    1oz (28g) liver
    extract

(4) *4oz (110g) casein*
    1oz (28g)
    lactalbumin
    1oz (28g)
    Equivite
    (pellets)
    2oz (56g)
    wheatgerm
    1oz (28g) gluten
    1oz (28g) robin
    red

With all recipes use up to 6 eggs or approx. 150ml water, adding dry ingredients to eggs in stages and mixing each stage well. Add colourings if necessary. With Mix (2) 5ml of flavouring and sweetener, etc., can be added if required. Mixes (1), (3) and (4) have a natural attraction and can be used unflavoured. Mix to a firm paste and roll into balls. Use within twenty-four hours or freeze and use within twenty-four hours of defrosting.

Rodney Chamberlain briefly admires a fast-growing mirror carp before it is released into a growing-on pond.

A cracking brace of common carp from a Cambridge syndicate lake.

These baits will be of great use in hard-fished waters, where the majority of anglers are attacking the problem with strongly flavoured HP baits, home-made or purchased ready-made, using flavours such as:

Regular Flavourings

Almond	Maple cream
Aniseed	Milk
Banana	Peanut
Butter	Peach
Caramel	Pineapple
Cinnamon	Sea fish
Cream	Strawberry
Fenugreek	Sweetcorn
Golden syrup	Tiger nut
Hazelnut	Toffee
Honey	Treacle
Liver	Turkish delight
Malt	Tuttifrutti
Maple	Walnut

Ethyl Alcohol Flavours

Black cherry	Juicy fruit
Bun spice zest	Red rum
Cherry top	Salmon
Cornish ice-cream	Sickly butter
Fresh pineapple	Strawberry jam
Fresh shrimp	Sweet plum

Use of flavours should be kept to a minimum, taking note of the concentration levels from individual suppliers. Add 5–10ml max. to a 1lb (450g) bait mix. Higher levels could become repellent. Add sweeteners to suitable flavours in doses of 5–10ml to 1lb (450g) of bait.

The secret with good home-made HNV baits is that if the correct base ingredients are chosen they may release a natural flavour which will not be of a repellent level. Even if you choose to add a flavour to your HNV bait make sure that it complements these natural releases and do not overdo the level. Keep it subtle – around five to ten millilitres per pound of bait – but take note of the supplier's recommendations as strengths vary from supplier to supplier. Probably of greater value to HNV baits than artificial flavours are natural oils, such as:

Bergamot oil	Geranium oil
Black pepper oil	Ginger oil
Cinnamon oil	Juniper berry oil
Clove oil	Peppermint oil
Garlic oil	Spearmint oil

These oils are available in 20ml glass dropper bottles from 'Nutrabaits'. Instructions for use are marked on the label. Each will require the use of an emulsifier, available in 100ml dropper bottles from the same source. Instructions again are on the label.

The use of these in a bait is more natural and more acceptable for long-term benefits. The quantity for use per pound of bait is, ideally, one to two millilitres. To get the benefit of release of the oils into the water there may be a need to add an emulsifier to the oil prior to mixing, so check with your supplier for the amount required, if necessary. Suppliers of bait ingredients, etc., can be found in the reference section at the back of this book (see page 125).

Boiled Baits

There is one more form of HP and HNV baits and that is the boiled bait. This has evolved to overcome the problem of the bait breaking down and dissolving which prevents long-term presentation of a bait, and to repel other species of fish which may suck at a paste bait and whittle it down to nothing without the angler knowing. To make the previous recipes into boilies use eggs rather than water or include an ingredient such as Nukamel. The obvious move is to use eggs as these do not alter the main ingredient mix, but Nukamel is one ingredient that will allow a good protein base mix to be made up. You will best decide what exactly the requirements of your bait are and use a mix to suit.

The methods of turning these mixtures into boiled baits will involve the use of a large saucepan filled with boiling water and a large flour sieve. The amount of time for boiling will vary to suit your requirement for skinned, firm or hard baits. Immersion of twenty to thirty baits in the boiling water for ten to thirty seconds will give lightly skinned baits, thirty seconds to one minute will give a firmly cooked bait, which will be moist and flexible (*see* Fig 39), and from one minute to

three minutes will give a hard dense bait which will survive for long periods.

Many of the pre-packed baits are of this well-boiled type. Release of flavours is restricted from boiled baits, and the longer the cooking the weaker the flavour is as it evaporates off. It is possible to boost this by adding a small amount of diluted flavouring from a spray-cap bottle to the bait once it is cooled, or even to the bait during thawing from the freezer. This will allow a short-term attraction boost after the baits enter the swim. Do not overdo this addition though as it can lead to repelling the carp instead of attracting it!

To make boiled baits buoyant, place them in a hot oven (approximately 375°F/190°C/

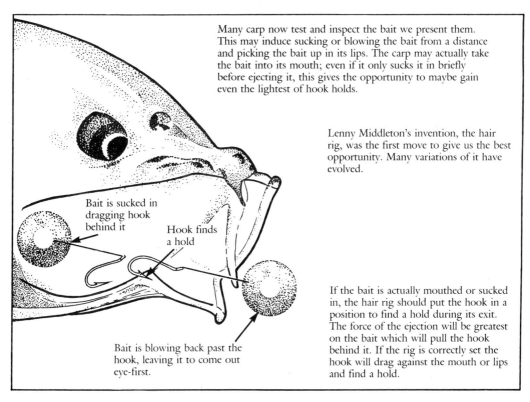

Many carp now test and inspect the bait we present them. This may induce sucking or blowing the bait from a distance and picking the bait up in its lips. The carp may actually take the bait into its mouth; even if it only sucks it in briefly before ejecting it, this gives the opportunity to maybe gain even the lightest of hook holds.

Lenny Middleton's invention, the hair rig, was the first move to give us the best opportunity. Many variations of it have evolved.

Bait is sucked in dragging hook behind it

Hook finds a hold

Bait is blowing back past the hook, leaving it to come out eye-first.

If the bait is actually mouthed or sucked in, the hair rig should put the hook in a position to find a hold during its exit. The force of the ejection will be greatest on the bait which will pull the hook behind it. If the rig is correctly set the hook will drag against the mouth or lips and find a hold.

Fig 39   View of bait ejection

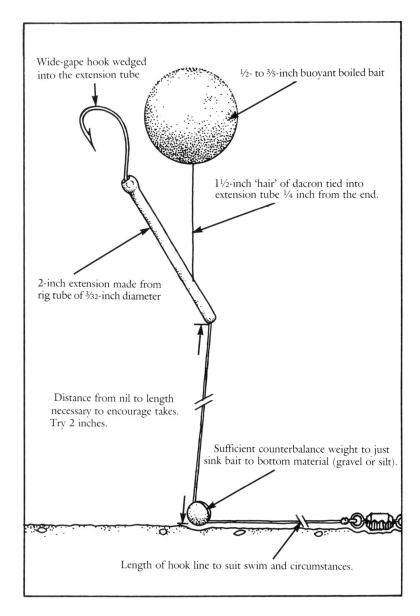

Wide-gape hook wedged into the extension tube

½- to ⅗-inch buoyant boiled bait

1½-inch 'hair' of dacron tied into extension tube ¼ inch from the end.

2-inch extension made from rig tube of ³⁄₃₂-inch diameter

Distance from nil to length necessary to encourage takes. Try 2 inches.

Sufficient counterbalance weight to just sink bait to bottom material (gravel or silt).

Length of hook line to suit swim and circumstances.

Fig 40   Extension rig with buoyant bait

Gas mark 5) for 10 to 15 minutes or in a microwave oven for 2 to 3 minutes. These buoyant baits can then be fished suspended a few inches or more off the bottom, clear of silt, weed or other debris, which the weight of the hook may pull your bait into while the free offerings sit on top. Fig 40 shows some applications for buoyant boiled baits.

Baked Baits

While some bait recipes did and still do attract and catch carp on the bottom of the various fisheries, there have been occasions when conditions have seen the fish feed off the bottom and then take surface baits. Any bait mix can be altered to become a floater to make your bait suitable for surface presentation; you need only adjust some ingredients and change the method of cooking from boiling to oven baking or microwave cooking. The ingredients change can be effected by taking out heavy ingredients, such as casein, and by substituting more sodium caseinate, and soya isolate instead of soya flour, etc. Here are two recipes for floater mixes:

(1) 4oz (110g) Munchies
3oz (85g) sodium caseinate
1oz (28g) gluten
½ tsp. baking powder

(2) 2oz (56g) casein
3oz (85g) soya flour
2oz (56g) sodium caseinate
1oz (28g) gluten
1oz (28g) Equivite (pellets)
½ tsp. baking powder

With both mixes 6–8 eggs will be required or, instead of making a full batch, place 4 eggs in a mixing bowl, add any flavourings and sweeteners required and whisk together.

If colouring is required add this to the dry mix. Slowly add the dry mixed ingredients to the eggs until a consistency of thick soup is achieved. Pour this into a greased baking tray and place in a pre-heated oven at 375°F/190°C/Gas mark 5 for twenty to thirty minutes until risen and sufficiently cooked. Remove and allow to cool.

The bait mix should be runny, not stiff as with paste baits. Whisk some air into this runny mixture, and bake in a flat, round or square baking tin until the mix rises. Experimenting with temperatures and times will be necessary to obtain the correct finished product. Grocery stores stock pre-measured bread, cake and batter mixes which you can use as a foundation for your floater mix. Once made up you can present the baits as shown in Figs 31 and 51 (pages 49 and 76).

PET FOOD AND CEREAL BAITS

To cover surface baits fully the ready-made pet food and breakfast cereals cannot be forgotten. Preoccupied feeding can be encouraged by introducing large quantities of these foods, liberally scattering them on the surface as free offerings prior to your hook-bait being introduced. A list of suitable floating baits can be found below.

Felix Crunch
Go-Cat
Kelloggs Golden Nuggets
Kelloggs Start cereal

Munchies
Pedigree Chum Mixer
Pedigree Chum Small-Bite Mixer
Purina Sea Nips

With the biscuit-type pet foods there is a difficulty in attaching them to the hook. This can be overcome by soaking them prior to use. To do this, place the amount you intend to use, perhaps 4oz (110g), into a plastic food box, and cover them briefly with boiling water. Pour the water off and seal the box. Shake the contents vigorously for a few minutes to prevent them sticking together. If you wish to boost the attraction or change the flavour, add 2ml of flavouring and sweetener to the container during the shaking. In a couple of hours the bait will be soft enough for easy hooking.

Little or no preparation is necessary for most types except with the harder varieties of biscuit which may require a brief wetting with water. This should be drained off immediately and followed by storage during transit, etc., in a flask or sealed polythene bag to make them moist and rubbery and ideal for hooking (see Fig 41).

Fig 41   Thermos jar for frozen bait storage

Where floaters have been used extensively and the fish have become wary the baits can be made more attractive and acceptable to them again by adding some of your flavourings to them. This can be done by adding a couple of millilitres to the polythene bag prior to putting in the moistened floaters. They will then carry the flavour, encouraging fresh interest. Choose a different flavour or attractor to the one you use in your bottom baits – a savoury surface bait if you use a sweet bottom bait, or vice versa.

It is worth considering using surface baits in your bottom-bait range. You can gain the benefits of biscuit-type baits which are good surface baits, by grinding them down to a fine meal and mixing them with a binder like gluten. Three recipes using pet foods as the bulk ingredients, enhanced where necessary with additional protein ingredients and attractors, are given below. These can be fished either as soft pastes, or as boiled baits by substituting the water with eggs in the mixing.

(1) *8oz (225g)*
     Munchies
     1oz (28g) sodium
     caseinate
     1oz (28g) gluten

(2) *6oz (170g) trout*
     pellets
     2oz (56g) sodium
     caseinate
     1oz (28g) soya
     flour
     1oz (28g) gluten

(3) *4oz (110g) Sluis*
     Universal
     4oz (110g) Sluis
     mynah food
     1oz (28g) sodium
     caseinate
     1oz (28g) gluten

Mix the above with 4–6 eggs, adding colourings, flavourings and sweeteners if you feel the need. Alternatively, leave the bait in its natural form and allow the base flavour to leach out. Roll the mix into baits of the size you require and boil for thirty seconds to two minutes to obtain the hardness you require.

Finally, the limit on experimenting with ingredients will be set by the angler's own imagination. Many good books exist written by individual carp anglers who pass on some more technical and complex bait recipes including the use of amino acids, etc., and in the reference section at the end of this book you will find a list of recommended books you might wish to obtain.

6 Methods and Tactics

If we were to turn the clocks back twenty years or even only ten years carp fishing methods would be so different, but many of the old methods will still attract and catch carp today. As we have seen with the baits, there were many sound ideas then which caught a lot of good carp! The old methods that caught carp are still the same today in many ways; what has really happened is that thinking anglers have applied a great deal of effort to improving them, mainly to increase the catch rates as carp gradually became wary of the various methods employed. Some of these methods have never been refined or changed, being at their best as originally conceived.

Baits were altered from soft pastes through to boiled baits to overcome various problems and these new forms of bait in turn created difficulties requiring some alterations and improvements in method to present them to their best effect. In the halcyon days of carp fishing the only real thing the prospective carp angler had to overcome was the natural wariness the carp had for unnatural food! Today the whole gambit has changed, and carp anglers old and new are pitting their wits and experience against 'educated' carp that may well have seen almost every bait or rig devised in one form or another.

It is necessary to have an open mind and experience of many methods to enable any opportunity that arises to be capitalised on. So much can affect the chances we have to catch carp on any water: conditions change with the seasons, and from day to day the prevailing weather conditions will also affect the carps' environment. The presentation may have to be altered or possibly a different swim fished, as the carp may have moved.

Some carp anglers are obsessed with obtaining the maximum distance of cast under any circumstance, on big open waters and even on the small secluded lakes and pits. Others go to great lengths to equip

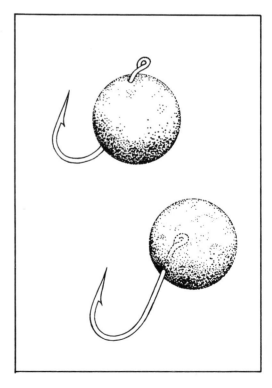

Fig 42   Eye- and side-hooked boiled baits (bolt rig)

A beautiful mirror carp of 3lb from a small town-centre lake.

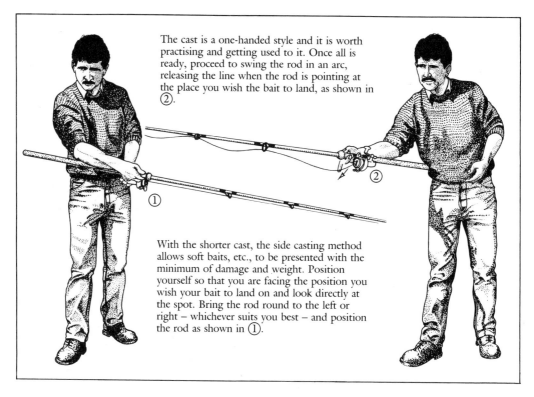

The cast is a one-handed style and it is worth practising and getting used to it. Once all is ready, proceed to swing the rod in an arc, releasing the line when the rod is pointing at the place you wish the bait to land, as shown in ②.

With the shorter cast, the side casting method allows soft baits, etc., to be presented with the minimum of damage and weight. Position yourself so that you are facing the position you wish your bait to land on and look directly at the spot. Bring the rod round to the left or right – whichever suits you best – and position the rod as shown in ①.

Fig 43   Side cast for short range

themselves with all the latest technology in tackle which will allow them to place a bait at a distance between one hundred and one hundred and fifty yards. They then go along and fish a water that may only be an acre in size so everything is out of balance and out of character with the swim being fished. Tactics need consideration to allow each water to be exploited to the full. Do not just slavishly copy the ideas here, but experiment! Use a standard rig on one rod and try an improved or modified one on the second rod or third, if your local club or fishery owner and water authority allow the use of three rods.

The following methods will help you get started. Where possible, each method will be related to where it can be most useful, though you may be able to find other uses for them.

We will start with the close-range methods and tactics using all the various bait types listed. Not every bait will be detailed but the principal ones of each category will be covered.

CLOSE-RANGE CASTING

Short, close-range fishing is probably the hardest for most carp anglers, new and old, to come to terms with. On even the largest waters the fish patrol and feed in the margins, locating the free offerings thrown in by departing anglers, and anything falling from bank-side vegetation, fruits and seeds from trees, and any larvae and insects doing the same! On many deep pits and quarries the only location for food accumulations may be

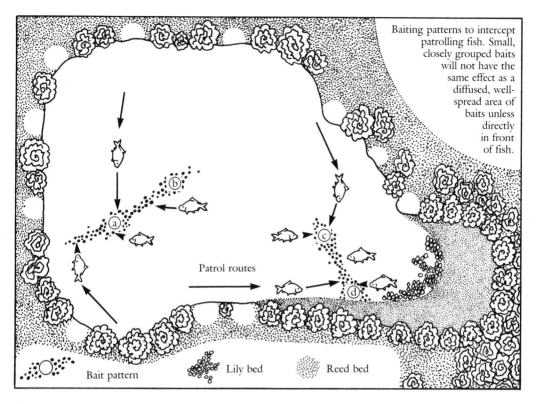

Baiting patterns to intercept patrolling fish. Small, closely grouped baits will not have the same effect as a diffused, well-spread area of baits unless directly in front of fish.

Patrol routes

Bait pattern   Lily bed   Reed bed

Fig 44   Bait pattern for margin and mid-range patrolling fish

in the margins, all other areas of water being very deep with little or no natural feeding areas. It is very hard for some anglers simply to drop a bait a few feet from the bank, but the ability to recognise when to do so can provide an extra opportunity to catch. Many long-casting anglers actually cast to the far side margins, but will never try the margins at their feet. The exploiting of far bank margins is not something that can be ignored especially if that bank is private and out of bounds – it is naturally a safe area for carp to retreat to. Special methods exist to deal with the far bank margins (*see* page 93).

Rigs and Baits

Side-Hooked and Hair-Rigged Bait

With close-range and margin fishing the most important thing to remember is to be quiet and invisible to patrolling or feeding carp. Even one stray noise like a dropped box or the banging in of bank sticks and brolly poles will spook the fish and put them off that particular area for some considerable time. The methods you use for close-range fishing can also have similar results, scaring away any fish that come into the swim. The worst offenders in margin fishing are probably tight lines which may foul on the fins or tail of upturned feeding fish, usually noticeable by jerky twitches of line at the rod top or the indicator followed by a swirl and bow wave

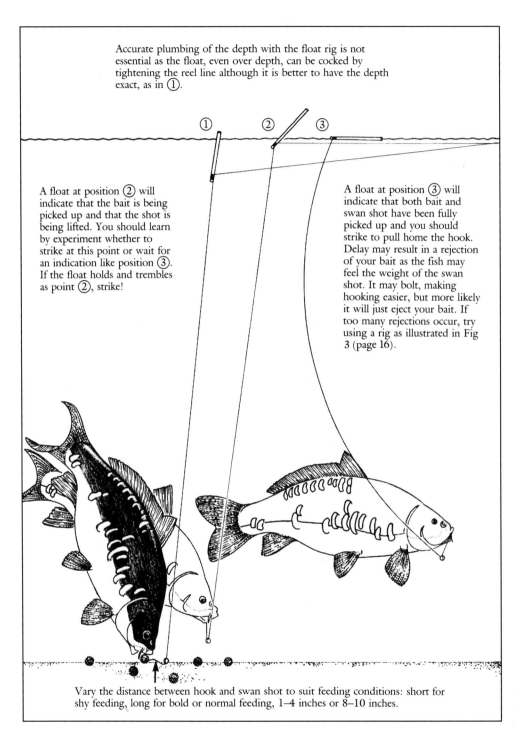

Accurate plumbing of the depth with the float rig is not essential as the float, even over depth, can be cocked by tightening the reel line although it is better to have the depth exact, as in ①.

A float at position ② will indicate that the bait is being picked up and that the shot is being lifted. You should learn by experiment whether to strike at this point or wait for an indication like position ③. If the float holds and trembles as point ②, strike!

A float at position ③ will indicate that both bait and swan shot have been fully picked up and you should strike to pull home the hook. Delay may result in a rejection of your bait as the fish may feel the weight of the swan shot. It may bolt, making hooking easier, but more likely it will just eject your bait. If too many rejections occur, try using a rig as illustrated in Fig 3 (page 16).

Vary the distance between hook and swan shot to suit feeding conditions: short for shy feeding, long for bold or normal feeding, 1–4 inches or 8–10 inches.

Fig 45   Float fishing for carp

as the carp vacates the swim. The methods to use in this case will be float fishing, free-lining or legering with slack lines to a fixed lead or even floating baits. The rigs and methods are illustrated in Figs 26, 36, 45 and 46.

Depending on the stage of carp angling tactics in use on the water in question you can use any variety of methods of presentation to suit the baits you may choose to fish with. The various terminal tackles shown in this chapter will allow you to choose a style to suit both the bait and the current stage of tactics on the chosen water or even to try something new. Probably the simplest of margin presentations is a free-line bait with just enough weight added to hold the line down away from the movements of the fish. This could be on a marginal shelf, or on the slope down to the bottom or hard on the bottom. If the opportunity presents itself, these baits can be observed; the carp can be seen taking one and then being hooked if you strike as it sucks in the bait. It is important when fishing like this to put only a few baits in the swim, such as boilies. Put five or six loose around your hookbait, with particles, and ten or twelve around your hook offering. When the hookbait is taken, start the strike as soon as you see the bait moving into the mouth. Do not wait, as the ejection will be over before you get the chance to set the hook! A side-hooked or hair-rigged bait is best for this style of fishing.

The same rig idea with a float added is illustrated in Fig 45. This can be any float you wish but a piece of peacock quill mounted on the line with silicon rubber is probably best. This can be fished close into the margins or onto close-in bars, etc. A long length of line between the hook and shot will ensure fin activity does not upset or scare off the feeding fish. Use a float to indicate what is happening when you cannot see the bait due to water

colour or when fishing in amongst weed beds or lilies. If the float is set to fish with worms, etc., set the float over depth with the shot closer to the hook to give good registration of the bite. Side-hooked or hair-rigged boiled, paste or particle baits, etc., can be used with this method; a handful of free offerings dropped in around the float or a bed of hemp or other small particles where the hookbait is to be fished can be used to attract the carp to feed.

Bolt Rigs

Fig 46 shows bait on a bolt rig for margin fishing. This can be boiled, paste or particle bait, again with a few free offerings or a bed of hemp or tiger nuts, etc., acting as an attractor. Note the lay of the reel line with the swan shot three feet above the terminal tackle to ensure that the slack line lies flat out of the way of the feeding fish. This type of rig can be used after dark in conjunction with indicators and open bail arms, to deal with the rapid take-off of the carp as it is hooked! Buoyant baits can also be used with this rig and with all the others if you choose (*see* Fig 47).

Fig 48 shows a bolt-rigged bait fished on a margin shelf; this may be along the bank to the left or right of where you will be positioned. The location of such feeding areas can be made by looking carefully at the margins to note any areas of clean gravel or bottom material where carp may have stopped to root around. When you find them or if you feel the carp visit the margins but no visible signs confirm it, you should deposit a small quantity of boiled baits or particles into the chosen areas, perhaps ten or twelve of either. Then check regularly to see if these disappear. Obviously the best time to do this sort of baiting is when you are fishing the chosen water for a period of at least

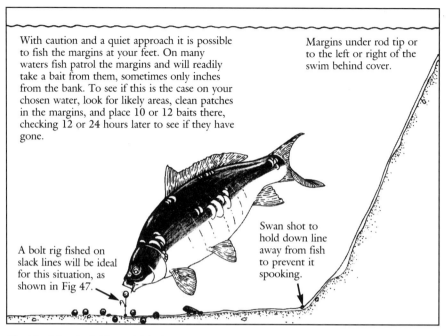

With caution and a quiet approach it is possible to fish the margins at your feet. On many waters fish patrol the margins and will readily take a bait from them, sometimes only inches from the bank. To see if this is the case on your chosen water, look for likely areas, clean patches in the margins, and place 10 or 12 baits there, checking 12 or 24 hours later to see if they have gone.

Margins under rod tip or to the left or right of the swim behind cover.

Swan shot to hold down line away from fish to prevent it spooking.

A bolt rig fished on slack lines will be ideal for this situation, as shown in Fig 47.

Fig 46   Margin fishing with bolt rig

twenty-four hours or when the water is sufficiently close for you to be able to visit it daily to check.

Once you have identified the best areas to present a bait, then the rig shown in Fig 49 will be the one to use. It consists of a fluted lead, chosen to prevent the bomb rolling off the shelf after you move along the bank to position the rod. The hookbait should be positioned *after* you have positioned the free offerings, again ten or twelve of these plus the hookbait. It is essential to count the number going in so that you can see if any are taken, and this applies to all margin methods.

The most important thing to remember with this method is that the line should be slack from the bomb to the rod tip, so position the swan shot three or four feet up the line. This will sink the line immediately below the bait and prevent contact with the fish when they move in to feed. Once you have positioned the baited hook exactly

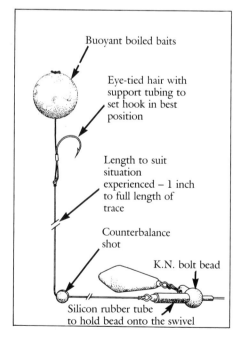

Buoyant boiled baits

Eye-tied hair with support tubing to set hook in best position

Length to suit situation experienced – 1 inch to full length of trace

Counterbalance shot

K.N. bolt bead

Silicon rubber tube to hold bead onto the swivel

Fig 47   Suspended bait bolt rig

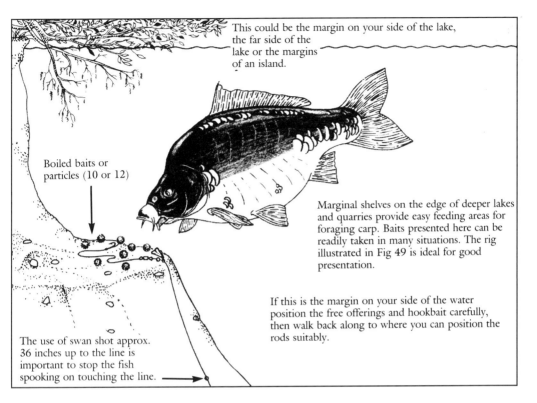

This could be the margin on your side of the lake, the far side of the lake or the margins of an island.

Boiled baits or particles (10 or 12)

Marginal shelves on the edge of deeper lakes and quarries provide easy feeding areas for foraging carp. Baits presented here can be readily taken in many situations. The rig illustrated in Fig 49 is ideal for good presentation.

If this is the margin on your side of the water position the free offerings and hookbait carefully, then walk back along to where you can position the rods suitably.

The use of swan shot approx. 36 inches up to the line is important to stop the fish spooking on touching the line.

Fig 48   Margin shelf presentation

where you require it, lower the bomb into a position to allow some slack line to give movement to the bait. The bomb can be semi-fixed to the trace to provide a bolt rig, or you can rely on the swan shot as a bolt back stop or use a power gum knot a few inches or so behind the bomb to give the bolt effect. Let out line from the reel and lay the swan shot straight down the shelf; then, paying out plenty of line, move along the bank to your swim and position the rod so that it points at the baited area. Sink the line and position the rod back into rests, attach your indicator, leaving the bail arm closed with the anti-reverse off, or the bail arm open, whichever is your preference, and await events!

Floating Bait

Staying with close-range fishing, but moving from bottom baits to surface or slow-sinking surface baits, we come to the use of floating baits such as bread, buoyant boilies, pet foods, etc. Fig 50 shows how to present these in the margins or at close range. There are various ways to fish floaters, from free-lining to the use of controllers. The latter are necessary to get baits into position over short distances, particularly with the smaller size lightweight surface baits.

A point that should be remembered with surface fishing at close range is the balancing of rod, line and clutch settings. Carp hooked at close range may take off at high speed and your tackle should be flexible enough to accommodate this. A stiff, heavy-actioned

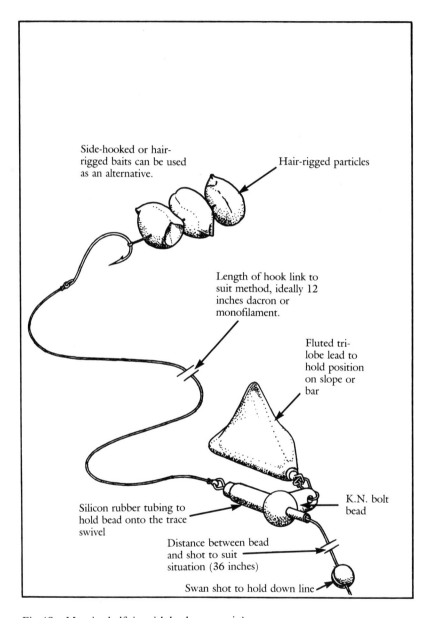

Side-hooked or hair-rigged baits can be used as an alternative.

Hair-rigged particles

Length of hook link to suit method, ideally 12 inches dacron or monofilament.

Fluted tri-lobe lead to hold position on slope or bar

Silicon rubber tubing to hold bead onto the trace swivel

K.N. bolt bead

Distance between bead and shot to suit situation (36 inches)

Swan shot to hold down line

Fig 49   Margin shelf rig with back stop weight

distance casting rod is not suitable for this; neither is a tight clutch and back winding to give line, at least not until you have gained experience and are using suitably balanced tackle. Fishing close to weed beds, lily beds or sunken snags, etc., may require the use of stepped-up compound taper rods, with lines of 15 or 18 pounds to stop and hold a big fish from snagging. However, this should be a last resort as serious damage can occur if too much pressure is applied unnecessarily.

In Figs 50, 51 and 26 we see the most basic form of surface fishing: floating crust. It can be fished in open water in gaps in the weed or lilies. As shown in Fig 51 it is free-lined, and this can be used with any floating bait that does not need to be presented too far

out. If crust is to be fished further out its weight can be increased by lightly dunking it into the water and quickly – but gently – casting out. Crust and any floating bait can also be fished below the surface at any depth, but particularly just below the surface; this will also defeat the waterfowl who cannot see it, but watch out for seagulls! A surface bait can be fished close in and suspended below the rod tip, on waters where fish have become wary of line; this can help catch night margin-feeding carp. The line is kept fairly tight by putting a light indicator on the line with at least eighteen inches of slack to allow the carp to take the bait well and turn to swim off. Close observation of the indicator is paramount in this situation.

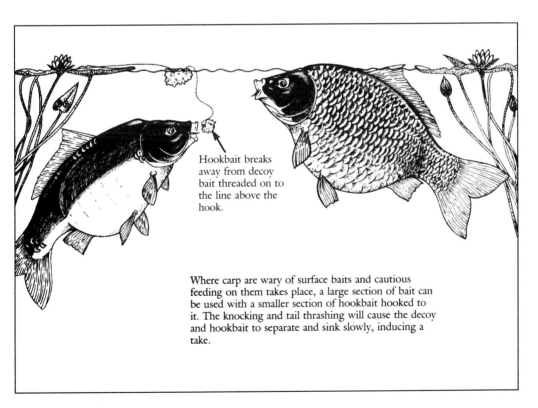

Hookbait breaks away from decoy bait threaded on to the line above the hook.

Where carp are wary of surface baits and cautious feeding on them takes place, a large section of bait can be used with a smaller section of hookbait hooked to it. The knocking and tail thrashing will cause the decoy and hookbait to separate and sink slowly, inducing a take.

Fig 50 Surface fishing with decoy bait

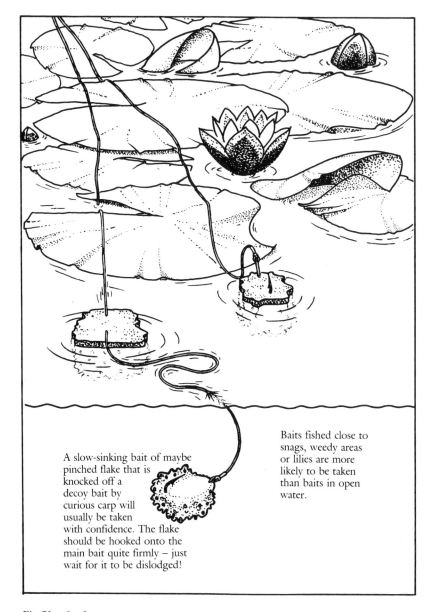

A slow-sinking bait of maybe pinched flake that is knocked off a decoy bait by curious carp will usually be taken with confidence. The flake should be hooked onto the main bait quite firmly – just wait for it to be dislodged!

Baits fished close to snags, weedy areas or lilies are more likely to be taken than baits in open water.

Fig 51   Surface presentation method

With the smaller, lighter floating baits some form of controller is necessary and in Fig 67 you will see an example of one of the most common types in use. With small particle floaters the important factor is to encourage feeding by liberal helpings of free offerings, and once this is achieved then the hook sample can be introduced. A light application of line grease in the form of Mucilin should be added to the line from rod to controller and from controller to within twelve inches of the bait. This applies to all surface methods, with the exception of the anchored methods which should not be greased at all, although there can be an exception when a little Mucilin may be added to the hooklength only.

With all surface methods ensure the carp have an adequate chance to recognise the bait as safe by giving plenty of free offerings before actually introducing the hookbait. Where the carp are wary of the regular surface baits try something different by changing the size and the colour, flavour or texture. With crust, attach a large piece a couple of inches up the line with a smaller piece mounted on the hook. Even try a piece of pinched flake which will only just float; when the carp swirls falsely at the bait this piece of flake might be taken as it may sink slowly and fool the wariest carp, as shown in Fig 51.

This slow-sinking bread flake can be very useful for stalking margin-patrolling carp. As the fish swims along, flick out a piece of pinched flake from a concealed position to flutter down in front of it; very often this will be taken immediately. In deep water where the take cannot be seen, hold a loop of line between your fingers for bite indication – as it is pulled out, strike firmly!

MEDIUM-RANGE CASTING

Progressing from margin-fished baits, we move on to medium-range methods and tactics. You will find that on many heavily fished waters the fish may not come within the marginal areas, particularly during day-light hours and will spend much time in 'safe' areas some distance from the anglers. On many waters that do not allow night fishing, carp have recognised that it is safe to come into the margins and shallow areas after the anglers have left. They then feed on all the free bait thrown in during the day, which they have hitherto ignored. The odd hour gained by slow packing up after dark on this sort of fishery has proved very productive. The secret is absolute quiet!

Mid-range methods can create difficulties as the choice of where and how to present a bait is as difficult here as with margin fishing, but by using the information on location and feeding habits likely areas will undoubtedly be identified. The tackle for this mid-distance may well be the same as you employed for margin fishing, depending on the sort of distances and conditions encountered. If you are fishing at the extreme range of seventy yards for example, you would probably benefit from stepping up the action of the rod (*see* the advice on rods and blanks in Chapter 4, page 34).

The methods you choose to use will depend on how and where the carp are feeding. They could be found on gravel bars, in gulleys, on gravel pits, around weed beds, islands, etc., in estate-type lakes, or perhaps patrolling on or just under the surface in warm bright conditions. The methods and tactics you might use are illustrated in Figs 47, 49, 53 and 55. They are variants really of methods for closer range but with added refinements to improve their effectiveness. It is strange how many carp anglers old and new

The most used and abused method of casting is the overhead cast, as shown here. Many people tend to position the rod to one side of their body or the other; they look at one spot and the bait lands to one side or the other and they wonder why! Accuracy is of paramount importance in carp fishing and to achieve this requires some commitment to casting with a proven style and using it correctly.

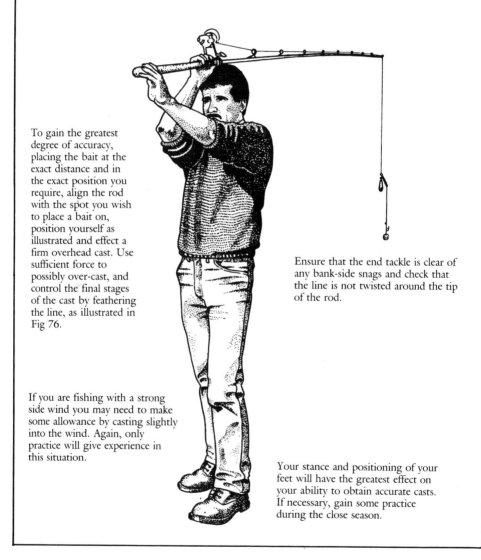

To gain the greatest degree of accuracy, placing the bait at the exact distance and in the exact position you require, align the rod with the spot you wish to place a bait on, position yourself as illustrated and effect a firm overhead cast. Use sufficient force to possibly over-cast, and control the final stages of the cast by feathering the line, as illustrated in Fig 76.

Ensure that the end tackle is clear of any bank-side snags and check that the line is not twisted around the tip of the rod.

If you are fishing with a strong side wind you may need to make some allowance by casting slightly into the wind. Again, only practice will give experience in this situation.

Your stance and positioning of your feet will have the greatest effect on your ability to obtain accurate casts. If necessary, gain some practice during the close season.

Fig 52   Overhead cast for medium to long range

A deep-bodied Italian-strain common carp of 24lb 8oz for Steve Frear, taken at close range.

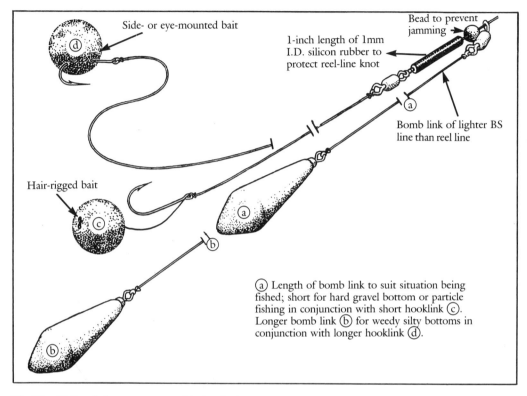

Side- or eye-mounted bait

Bead to prevent jamming →

1-inch length of 1mm I.D. silicon rubber to protect reel-line knot →

ⓐ

Bomb link of lighter BS line than reel line

Hair-rigged bait →

ⓒ

ⓐ

ⓑ

ⓑ

ⓐ Length of bomb link to suit situation being fished; short for hard gravel bottom or particle fishing in conjunction with short hooklink ⓒ. Longer bomb link ⓑ for weedy silty bottoms in conjunction with longer hooklink ⓓ.

Fig 53   Sliding link paternoster – side-hooked or hair-rigged

fail to come to terms with mid-range fishing, by using methods, etc., more in keeping with short-range or even long-range fishing. Adaptability is very important if you are to gain the benefits of fishing where the carp are feeding. Present a bait in that exact spot and you are guaranteed success; miss, and you may never catch!

Following the pattern of the close-range methods and tactics, we shall deal with the various leger methods and work up to surface methods.

Rigs and Baits

Leger Rigs

Fig 53 shows a typical basic leger rig using a sliding paternoster which is simple and uncomplicated and which will suit many of the day-to-day requirements of the legering angler. You may think that this method is outdated, but far from it – correct use of this particular method is still very productive and has only gone out of use in favour of modern methods due to the claims of *the* super rig having caught *the* fish. This paternoster rig might well have caught that same fish if the angler had been using it.

The rig illustrated in Fig 53 can be made

to suit various situations by adjustment of hooklink and bomb links. This could be from a long eighteen-inch hooklink for confidence rigs and shy carp to a short six-inch hooklink for bolt rigs where preoccupied, confident feeding takes place on particles, etc. Similarly, the bomb link can be varied to achieve a balance to this arrangement, with perhaps a twelve-inch bomb link or a two-inch link respectively or even a direct lead to reel line attachment for the bolt rig. The length of the bomb link can also be used to overcome the problems of a soft silty bottom or a weedy bottom, as detailed in Fig 54.

Shown in Fig 55 is another aid to fishing weedy, silty parts of the lake, particularly where extra weight may be necessary to achieve a cast to reach the desired spot. The buoyant leger link illustrated has many uses, but seems to be overlooked by many carp anglers today. In both cases the presentation should be with neutral or buoyant baits, or fished in conjunction with neutral density baits that will lie on the top of the weed or silt instead of being lost in it. Dense, heavy-mix baits may be lost in this way which may result in no activity, despite the bait being in a likely area, due to the flavour or attractor being rendered useless by saturation with the odour of rotting debris. Take a sniff at your bait immediately you retrieve it, to see if the flavour or attractor smell is being given off!

Balancing of buoyancy in baits can be achieved by using the lightest ingredients and by microwave cooking them, or by using ready-made buoyant boiled baits, etc. (see Chapter 5). Baits of either type should sink at a very slow rate to come to settle on or be suspended just off the surface of the bottom material. Hair-rigged baits are particularly useful in this situation. Another useful way of obtaining the slow descent of your bait is to attach a small cube or ball of polystyrene to the hook with PVA tape. This will pop up to

the surface indicating the exact position of your bait after the PVA dissolves and will allow the bait to settle on the bottom with an accumulation of slack line.

With the short-link paternoster used where preoccupied feeding takes place, the hair-rigged bait or side-hooked bait can be an advantage. The paternoster can be turned into a fixed paternoster by placing a bead and stop knot behind the bomb-link swivel, or you can use the rigs illustrated in Figs 47, 49 and 53.

Confidence Rigs

Other rigs for use with medium-range fishing are combinations of some of today's more sophisticated methods using various anti-tangle and confidence rigs and attachments designed to overcome the nervous, shy-biting carp, found on so many of our popular carp fisheries. It is worth at this point remembering the type of water you may be fishing. As outlined, the older-style paternoster rig is ideal for soft bottoms of estate-type lakes, and is usable on gravel pits. Some of the newer rigs are designed specifically for gravel-pit fishing over clean, gravelly bottoms, no allowance being made for silt and weed. Much of this is not found on gravel bars, the most common feature of gravel pits. Many of the newer gravel pits that are being stocked with carp are so new that they have very little in the way of silt deposits or weed beds, even in the gulleys.

If you take a look at the assortment of terminal tackles, you will see many different methods of tackling up with bolt or confidence rigs. They have one thing in common and that is, the lead is directly attached to the line, in fact with it running through the tubed centre (see Fig 56) or attached to a link bead attached to the line – no two-inch or twelve-inch bomb links here!

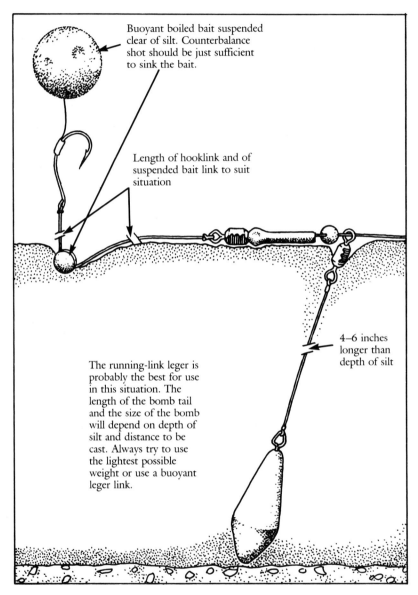

Buoyant boiled bait suspended clear of silt. Counterbalance shot should be just sufficient to sink the bait.

Length of hooklink and of suspended bait link to suit situation

4–6 inches longer than depth of silt

The running-link leger is probably the best for use in this situation. The length of the bomb tail and the size of the bomb will depend on depth of silt and distance to be cast. Always try to use the lightest possible weight or use a buoyant leger link.

Fig 54 Long sliding paternoster in silt

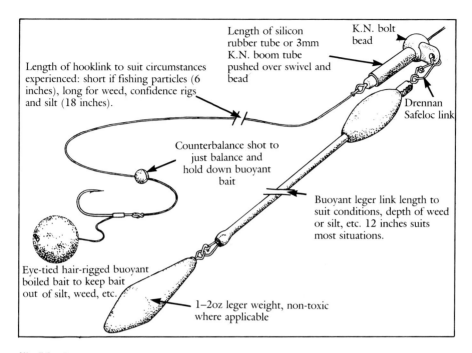

Length of silicon rubber tube or 3mm K.N. boom tube pushed over swivel and bead

K.N. bolt bead

Length of hooklink to suit circumstances experienced: short if fishing particles (6 inches), long for weed, confidence rigs and silt (18 inches).

Drennan Safeloc link

Counterbalance shot to just balance and hold down buoyant bait

Buoyant leger link length to suit conditions, depth of weed or silt, etc. 12 inches suits most situations.

Eye-tied hair-rigged buoyant boiled bait to keep bait out of silt, weed, etc.

1–2oz leger weight, non-toxic where applicable

Fig 55   Buoyant leger and buoyant bait for weed and silt

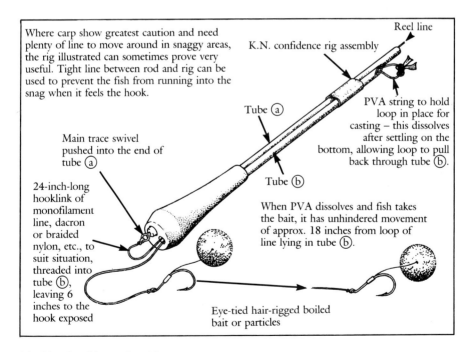

Where carp show greatest caution and need plenty of line to move around in snaggy areas, the rig illustrated can sometimes prove very useful. Tight line between rod and rig can be used to prevent the fish from running into the snag when it feels the hook.

Reel line

K.N. confidence rig assembly

Tube (a)

PVA string to hold loop in place for casting – this dissolves after settling on the bottom, allowing loop to pull back through tube (b).

Main trace swivel pushed into the end of tube (a)

Tube (b)

24-inch-long hooklink of monofilament line, dacron or braided nylon, etc., to suit situation, threaded into tube (b), leaving 6 inches to the hook exposed

When PVA dissolves and fish takes the bait, it has unhindered movement of approx. 18 inches from loop of line lying in tube (b).

Eye-tied hair-rigged boiled bait or particles

Fig 56   Confidence rig with PVA

Many will not perform to the design concept in weedy, silty conditions.

Fig 57 shows a gravel bar being fished with an anti-tangle rig; this could also be *any* rig not using anti-tangle tubes. Note the marker float showing the exact point of the bar for accurate bait positioning; it is important to obtain this accuracy with both the hookbait and the loose feed. One great idea that came into use in the early 1980s was the 'stringer', carrying say five or six free offerings in close proximity to the hookbait both during the cast and more importantly when the rig settles, next to the bait on the bottom (*see* Fig 58). The secret when using this rig is not to move the baited hook once it has settled, to ensure all the free baits stay close to the hook-

bait. The stringer can also be used without a hooklink to aid accurate positioning of the remaining free offerings and to avoid the attentions of the cute little feathered bait thieves who seem to have taken up residence on just about every carp water in the country. Fig 59 shows an alternative method of making up this feeder rig.

Looking back to Fig 42, you will see the line is following the contours of the bottom, aided by the addition of a swan shot, mounted on fine-bore silicon rubber some three feet up the reel line. The line can be taken tight from the bomb as shown in Fig 60 but this has arguable advantages and definite disadvantages. The disadvantage illustrated here is that feeding fish or

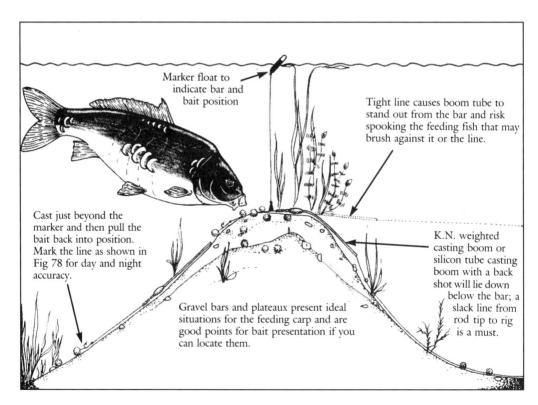

Marker float to indicate bar and bait position

Tight line causes boom tube to stand out from the bar and risk spooking the feeding fish that may brush against it or the line.

Cast just beyond the marker and then pull the bait back into position. Mark the line as shown in Fig 78 for day and night accuracy.

K.N. weighted casting boom or silicon tube casting boom with a back shot will lie down below the bar; a slack line from rod tip to rig is a must.

Gravel bars and plateaux present ideal situations for the feeding carp and are good points for bait presentation if you can locate them.

Fig 57   Gravel bar fished with slack line and boom

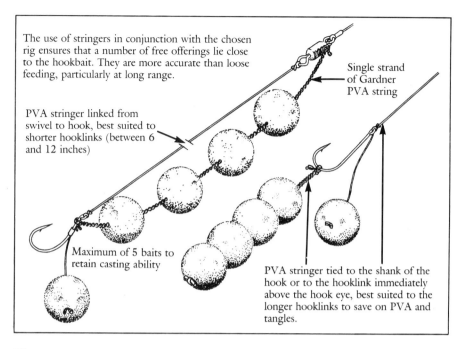

The use of stringers in conjunction with the chosen rig ensures that a number of free offerings lie close to the hookbait. They are more accurate than loose feeding, particularly at long range.

PVA stringer linked from swivel to hook, best suited to shorter hooklinks (between 6 and 12 inches)

Single strand of Gardner PVA string

Maximum of 5 baits to retain casting ability

PVA stringer tied to the shank of the hook or to the hooklink immediately above the hook eye, best suited to the longer hooklinks to save on PVA and tangles.

Fig 58 PVA stringers

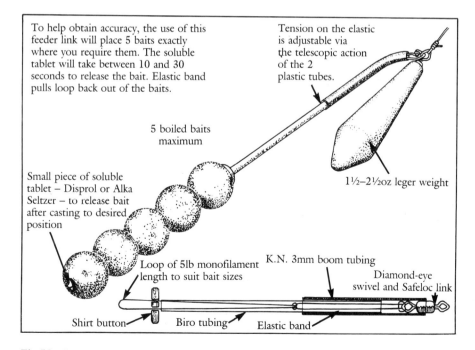

To help obtain accuracy, the use of this feeder link will place 5 baits exactly where you require them. The soluble tablet will take between 10 and 30 seconds to release the bait. Elastic band pulls loop back out of the baits.

Tension on the elastic is adjustable via the telescopic action of the 2 plastic tubes.

5 boiled baits maximum

Small piece of soluble tablet – Disprol or Alka Seltzer – to release bait after casting to desired position

1½–2½oz leger weight

Loop of 5lb monofilament length to suit bait sizes

K.N. 3mm boom tubing

Diamond-eye swivel and Safeloc link

Shirt button   Biro tubing   Elastic band

Fig 59 Long-range feeder rig

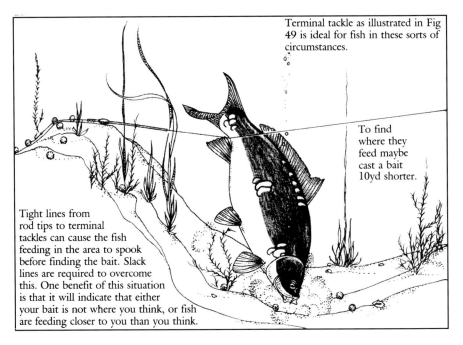

Terminal tackle as illustrated in Fig 49 is ideal for fish in these sorts of circumstances.

To find where they feed maybe cast a bait 10yd shorter.

Tight lines from rod tips to terminal tackles can cause the fish feeding in the area to spook before finding the bait. Slack lines are required to overcome this. One benefit of this situation is that it will indicate that either your bait is not where you think, or fish are feeding closer to you than you think.

Fig 60   Tight line from gravel bar

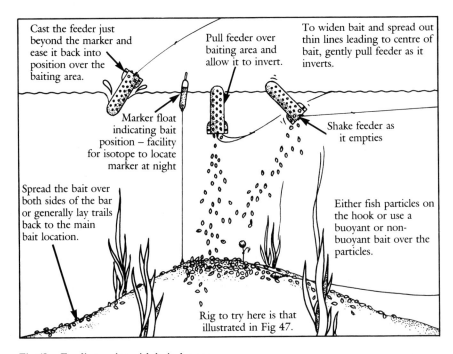

Cast the feeder just beyond the marker and ease it back into position over the baiting area.

Pull feeder over baiting area and allow it to invert.

To widen bait and spread out thin lines leading to centre of bait, gently pull feeder as it inverts.

Marker float indicating bait position – facility for isotope to locate marker at night

Shake feeder as it empties

Spread the bait over both sides of the bar or generally lay trails back to the main bait location.

Either fish particles on the hook or use a buoyant or non-buoyant bait over the particles.

Rig to try here is that illustrated in Fig 47.

Fig 61   Feeding swim with bait dropper

patrolling fish moving between bait and rod may give false indications and may well spook the fish out of the swim. It may also indicate that you are casting *past* the feeding fish and if the activity continues it may be worth placing one or more baits at shorter range.

Particle Bait

So far, the use of boiled or similar baits, and pastes has been covered. The other methods available include getting the carp preoccupied and feeding confidently. As already discussed, this will involve the use of particle baits, either baits like peanuts, hemp, chick peas, and maple peas, to name a few, or the mini-boilies now available. Whichever you choose the requirements with particles are the same: you will get the best possible results by putting the bait in a known feeding area. However, the use of particles can induce feeding out of normal areas by virtue of the attractiveness of a large volume of easily gained free food. The important point is the bait must be on a patrol route used by the carp. If it is, you may be lucky enough to draw stray fish in with bait placed in a strange area but the success may be short-lived and less than could be expected if the bait was presented correctly.

When fishing particles at range we must bear in mind the reason for their success – the attraction of large quantities of bait in a small area. To achieve accuracy of location you can use a marker as in Fig 42, but you will still require a great deal of bait in the swim. A catapult may get bait to the closer swims but a fair amount of it will end up scattered around, reducing the effect. What is necessary is some means of getting large quantities of bait to the required swim. Figs 34 and 61 show the method of getting particles in quantity to the distance required. The bulk feeder used, the 'Bait Rocket', is made by

Gardner Tackle, and is illustrated in Fig 62. There is a need for a suitably powerful casting rod to launch a fully loaded dropper of this size; a 2½-pound test curve, through-actioned rod will suit, matched with a 15-pound BS line. The sorts of rig to use with these particle methods are the short-link paternoster in a bolt-rig mode with short hook and bomb links (*see* Fig 53) or a more recent semi-fixed lead bolt rig as detailed in Fig 63. Whichever you decide to use, refer back to ensure you choose the correct combination of hooklink and lead configuration, remembering the difficulties experienced with dacron or braided nylon on some casting rigs.

Surface and Sub-Surface Bait

The final method for mid-range work is surface or sub-surface fishing with buoyant boiled baits, floating pastes or floaters, including bread crust. As with the other methods discussed, some form of weight will be necessary to allow the light baits to be fished effectively amongst feeding, patrolling carp. Where pressure from short-range surface fishing has pushed carp out beyond free-line surface presentation, several alternative methods exist. Figs 65 and 67 illustrate just some of the variations available.

Fig 64 details the original method to be used, created simply by adding a suitable size of leger weight to the free-line floater rig. For maximum efficiency, use a large Drennan brass ring linked to a bomb with a snap link, as illustrated. A large-diameter floating bead is placed between the ring and the hook; no other means of arresting the bomb is necessary. The bait is mounted on the hook, the size of which will depend on the bait, but a size 2 may be ideal with a large piece of bread crust. A large buoyant boiled bait could be used in conjunction with a side-hooking rig or a hair rig.

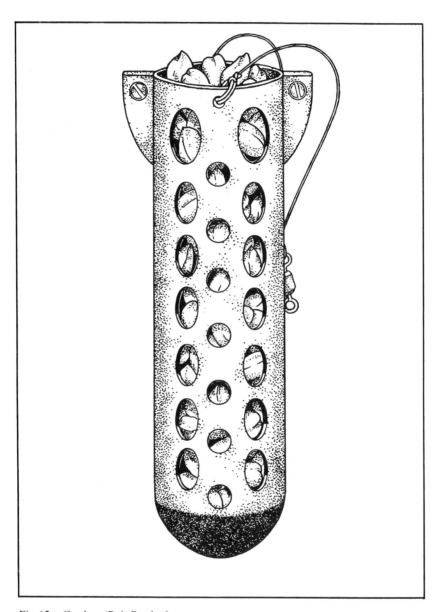

Fig 62   Gardner 'Bait Rocket'

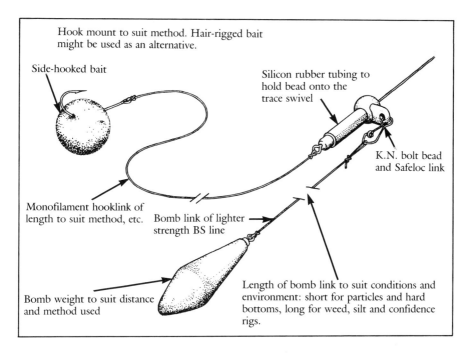

Fig 63   Semi-fixed paternoster

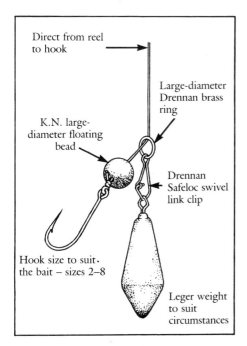

Fig 64   Floater casting rig

After casting, line is played out to allow the bait to come to the surface; alternatively, the bait can be suspended just under the surface if waterfowl are a nuisance or if you are offering a different bait to the carp. The advantage of this tethered floating bait is that you can position your bait in a given area and hold it there in wind or current. It will be particularly useful if you locate an area where the carp will more readily respond to a surface bait. Very often surface baits well .out from the normal range are freely taken.

The other methods of surface fishing are related to moving and untethered surface baits, typically cat and dog food, biscuits, home-made floaters based on boiled-bait ingredients, or even simple bread crust, etc. Fig 65 shows two methods of presentation using what are commonly known as controllers – weighted, floating bodies fished with the line running through the top. There are many versions of this useful device; the smaller one illustrated is the 'original' John Wilson 'Ten Pin'. This comes in two sizes to allow flexibility in use, for short- to medium-range and medium- to long-range surface particle fishing. Large quantities of particles are introduced upwind of the feeding area to obtain a degree of preoccupation and subsequent confident feeding. The hookbait and controller are then presented amongst a smaller quantity of free offerings allowed to drift into the feeding area on the wind.

The other controller, illustrated in Fig 66, is the Gardner 'Mixer Fixer'. The idea is the same as the 'Ten Pin' but it also carries its own supply of free samples to the exact hookbait area. It is ideal when there is no wind or there are obstacles like lily beds to obstruct

the drift of catapult-introduced free offerings. The fixer is designed to operate specifically with buoyant baits like Pedigree Chum Mixer or the smaller floating boiled baits. The free offerings, approximately two pouch loads, are held in the tube body during the cast and these automatically float free around the hook offering, after the fixer lands in the water. When using either of these controller feeders you should tackle up as illustrated in Fig 67 with either a swivel or leger stop to set the length of the hook link. If you use a swivel it is an idea to make it buoyant with the addition of a piece of Evode 'Float-a-Bait' wrapped around it, as illustrated in Fig 65.

A useful material for floater hooklinks using a swivel is waxed dental floss which

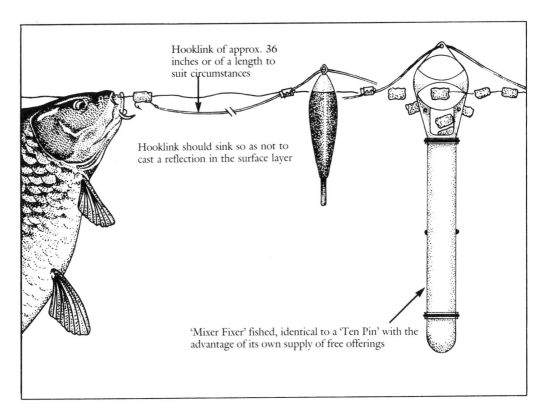

Hooklink of approx. 36 inches or of a length to suit circumstances

Hooklink should sink so as not to cast a reflection in the surface layer

'Mixer Fixer' fished, identical to a 'Ten Pin' with the advantage of its own supply of free offerings

Fig 65   Floating bait controllers

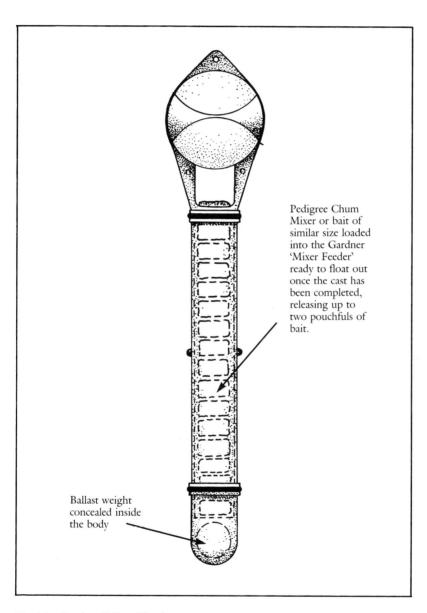

Pedigree Chum
Mixer or bait of
similar size loaded
into the Gardner
'Mixer Feeder'
ready to float out
once the cast has
been completed,
releasing up to
two pouchfuls of
bait.

Ballast weight
concealed inside
the body

Fig 66   Gardner 'Mixer Fixer'

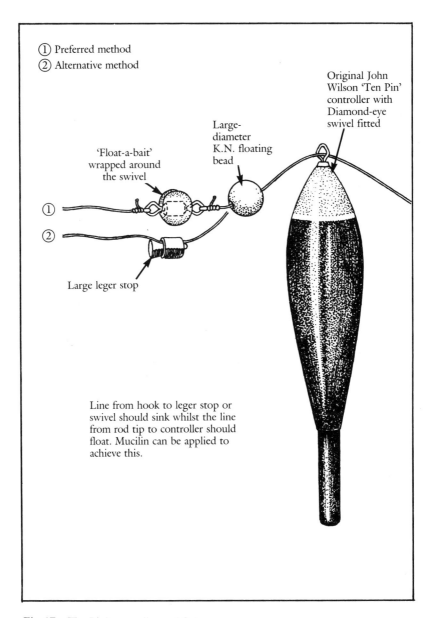

① Preferred method
② Alternative method

Original John Wilson 'Ten Pin' controller with Diamond-eye swivel fitted

Large-diameter K.N. floating bead

'Float-a-bait' wrapped around the swivel

①

②

Large leger stop

Line from hook to leger stop or swivel should sink whilst the line from rod tip to controller should float. Mucilin can be applied to achieve this.

Fig 67 'Ten Pin' controller and fixings

usually has a breaking strain of around 12 pounds. The texture of this material makes it less conspicuous than dacron or monofilament line, although monofilament line is probably a more suitable alternative. Grease, typically Mucilin, can be used to make the hooklink float but this will depend on whether the floating line is identified by the carp as dangerous and on how heavy the surface fishing on the given water has been. If the fish are shying off at the sight of the line on the surface try an ungreased hooklink or a longish hooklink with just several short areas of grease applied, allowing some sections to sink and some to float. This may just confuse and deceive the carp enough to induce a take when all else fails.

If no controllers are available one very basic floater rig can be made up by slipping a leger stop or swivel onto the line and moulding a good-sized piece of Evode 'Float-a-bait' around it – this is something you should always have in your tackle bag! It is very effective and very practical in weedy conditions where more solid controllers might snag, resulting in a lost fish. When a take occurs with any floater do not over-react and strike too early, but hold back and make certain the bait is taken and the line is tightening or is moving before striking. An early strike may spook your fish and any others that may be in the vicinity, curtailing any future activity!

LONG-RANGE CASTING

Finally we have come to what seems to be the most used method, that of long-range fishing. It seems that many carp anglers relate only to this method possibly because the discussions on tactics and methods today, in magazine articles, etc., are mainly about how far to cast and how to arrange the author's

own type of long-range rig. Or perhaps it is because many of the anglers who have taken up carp fishing have witnessed the more experienced anglers fishing at long range only and have not been around when they were margin or bar fishing to the extent that they have become blinkered and slavishly follow trends. The reason it has become necessary to cast in excess of one hundred yards is because of pressure and when a water is being fished hard then the pressure is at its greatest. By late summer the number of anglers has diminished and it can be possible to find the carp coming back into the margins to feed more frequently as they always have done when undisturbed by the angling fraternity.

Accepting then that long-range fishing is going to be necessary, we must approach it in exactly the same way as we have with all the previous methods, with a balance in tackle and tactics. The rod's test curve and action must match the correct breaking strain monofilament line and finally the terminal tackle, balancing the materials with the method.

For medium to long ranges of seventy to eighty yards, an ordinary overhead cast will normally serve adequately well. However, in windy conditions or where accuracy and perhaps longer casts are needed, an improved overhead cast is required. The sequence of actions illustrated in Figs 68, 69, 70 and 71 shows how you can obtain the desired results with a modified overhead cast. With practice, you should gain both distance and accuracy quite easily.

To achieve the optimum response from the rod's power curve, it must be loaded and compressed. Many casting styles do not come anywhere near the level possible if the correct technique and weight are combined. With many anglers most of their effort is wasted in getting the leger weight moving, the rod only being half compressed by the time they get

A classic-shaped mirror carp with near-linear markings taken during a glorious autumn day.

A beautiful example of a leather carp of 8lb for Darren Cowle.

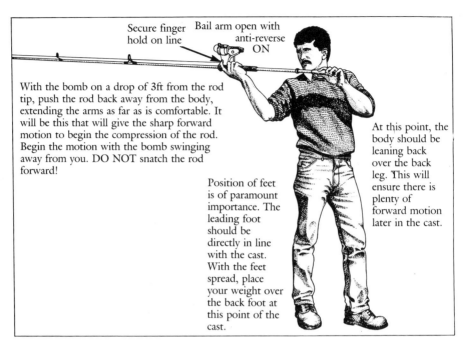

Secure finger
hold on line

Bail arm open with
anti-reverse
ON

With the bomb on a drop of 3ft from the rod tip, push the rod back away from the body, extending the arms as far as is comfortable. It will be this that will give the sharp forward motion to begin the compression of the rod. Begin the motion with the bomb swinging away from you. DO NOT snatch the rod forward!

At this point, the body should be leaning back over the back leg. This will ensure there is plenty of forward motion later in the cast.

Position of feet is of paramount importance. The leading foot should be directly in line with the cast. With the feet spread, place your weight over the back foot at this point of the cast.

Fig 68   Long-range casting   1

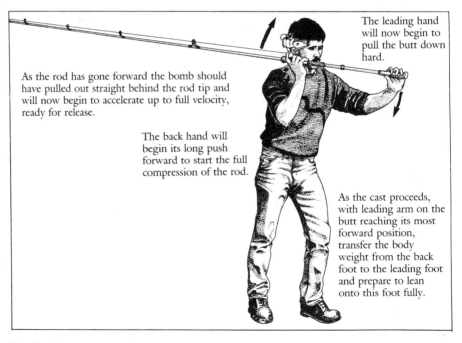

The leading hand will now begin to pull the butt down hard.

As the rod has gone forward the bomb should have pulled out straight behind the rod tip and will now begin to accelerate up to full velocity, ready for release.

The back hand will begin its long push forward to start the full compression of the rod.

As the cast proceeds, with leading arm on the butt reaching its most forward position, transfer the body weight from the back foot to the leading foot and prepare to lean onto this foot fully.

Fig 69   Long-range casting   2

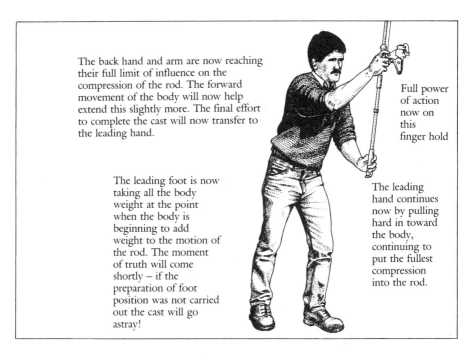

The back hand and arm are now reaching their full limit of influence on the compression of the rod. The forward movement of the body will now help extend this slightly more. The final effort to complete the cast will now transfer to the leading hand.

Full power of action now on this finger hold

The leading foot is now taking all the body weight at the point when the body is beginning to add weight to the motion of the rod. The moment of truth will come shortly – if the preparation of foot position was not carried out the cast will go astray!

The leading hand continues now by pulling hard in toward the body, continuing to put the fullest compression into the rod.

Fig 70   Long-range casting   3

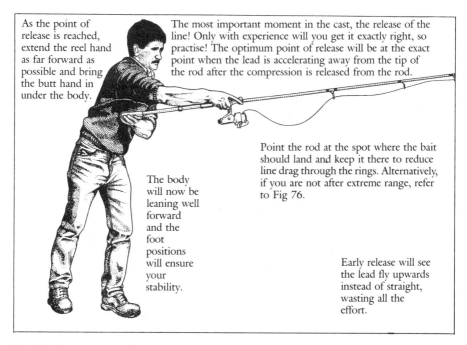

As the point of release is reached, extend the reel hand as far forward as possible and bring the butt hand in under the body.

The most important moment in the cast, the release of the line! Only with experience will you get it exactly right, so practise! The optimum point of release will be at the exact point when the lead is accelerating away from the tip of the rod after the compression is released from the rod.

The body will now be leaning well forward and the foot positions will ensure your stability.

Point the rod at the spot where the bait should land and keep it there to reduce line drag through the rings. Alternatively, if you are not after extreme range, refer to Fig 76.

Early release will see the lead fly upwards instead of straight, wasting all the effort.

Fig 71   Long-range casting   4

A mid-double mirror carp with the classic colouring, from a club fishery, taken at long range.

A midsummer 18lb mirror carp taken from a gravel pit at extreme range at midday.

the cast to the release point, resulting in a shorter than desired distance.

The secret of obtaining the maximum power from the cast to gain the required distance and accuracy, is to have the lead on the move with the reel line tight, before the compression of the rod commences. Figs 68, 69, 70 and 71 show how you can achieve this in a confined area, like the average swim. The lead and bait are accelerated from a slight back swing by swiftly pulling the rod forward, as in Fig 68, which ensures that by the time the rod reaches its start of compression some degree of this already exists. The compression builds to 100 per cent as the cast continues, right up until you reach the release point when the weight has

travelled through its full arc, past the tip. As the compression is released, the lead accelerates to full velocity and leaves the tip on its way to the distance you require.

Rigs and Baits

To achieve distance is one thing, but to effect good bait presentation along with it requires a great deal of understanding of the method in use and the ability to control the two when combined. Illustrated within the text here are methods in terminal tackle, casting and ideas to overcome some of the problems associated with obtaining as good as possible, if not perfect bait presentation. It is of no use sitting behind rods on which the bait and

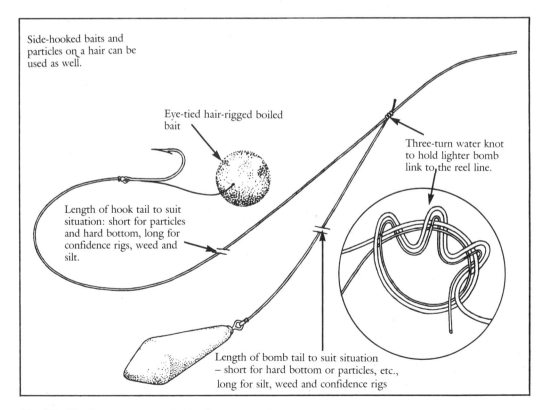

Side-hooked baits and particles on a hair can be used as well.

Eye-tied hair-rigged boiled bait

Three-turn water knot to hold lighter bomb link to the reel line.

Length of hook tail to suit situation: short for particles and hard bottom, long for confidence rigs, weed and silt.

Length of bomb tail to suit situation – short for hard bottom or particles, etc., long for silt, weed and confidence rigs

Fig 72   Fixed paternoster – Water knot secured

terminal tackle are completely useless due to tangles. All you may have to show over a whole weekend session could be a series of twitches instead of fish on the bank!

Paternosters

A basic paternoster is illustrated in Fig 72. It could be a sliding paternoster or even a fixed paternoster; either way it has been used a great deal in the past with considerable success. Providing it is used with monofilament line on both hooklinks and bomb links, tangling during the cast will be minimal. If you use material like dacron or braided nylon, etc., the chance of tangles will increase. This is why so much effort has gone into

developing today's anti-tangle rigs, or at least that is what they are supposed to be, but if incorrectly used they are no better than any other method!

To gain the extreme distances required on some fisheries to place baits amongst feeding fish, there is a need for heavy weights to be used. Bombs of 1½ or 2 ounces are quite common on bolt rigs, even for margin fishing, but it may be necessary to go up to 3 ounces or so to get over one hundred yards with bait and into the wind. The balance in rod and line will need to be good with up to 2½- to 2¾-pound test-curve rods and 15- to 18-pound BS line. The drag on such large-diameter lines will greatly reduce the distance of the cast. The way to overcome this drag is

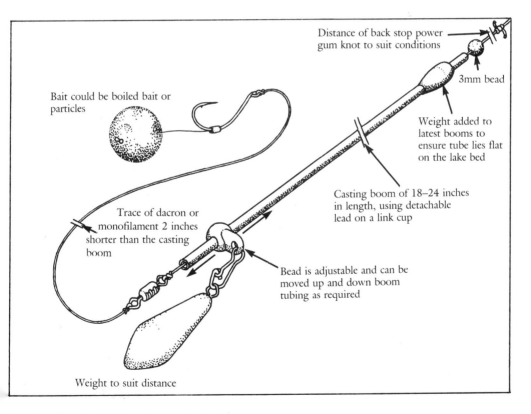

Fig 73   Casting boom with swivel or bead

to use a shock leader of 18-pound line, the length being approximately ten yards. To allow a reasonable amount of this line to be on the spool during the cast, the remaining reel line can be between 9 and 11 pounds. It is possible to use lighter lines but it would be unwise to do so until you have gained some experience of the waters you will fish, the problems being damage from snags, weed beds and gravel bars, etc. Fig 18 shows how to attach a shock leader to the reel line.

With the fixed paternoster and a heavy bomb you generally have a confidence rig and bolt rig combined. Once the free play on the hooklink and bomb link are taken up, the heavy bomb will cause the hook to prick the fish and find a hook hold.

Anti-Tangle Rigs

Moving on to some of today's anti-tangle rigs you will see illustrated in Fig 73 probably the original anti-tangle rig. This consists of a long, rigid or flexible plastic tube with originally a swivel pushed onto it, followed by specifically manufactured plastic beads that fit snugly onto the tubing. From this evolved the casting boom illustrated in Fig 74, with the lead weight mounted on the tubing, thus making it far more aerodynamic, allowing longer casts to be made.

Though these two designs are still available and are still useful, they have given way to more sophisticated designs where the bead type is available in a smaller version, and which

24lb 8oz of Italian-strain common carp from a small gravel pit.

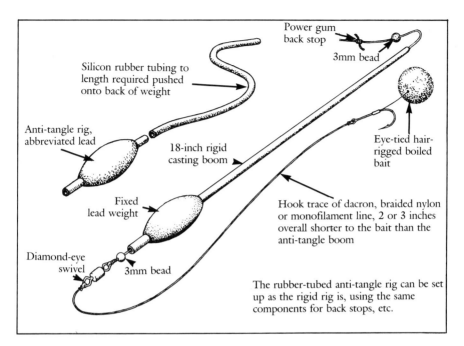

Power gum back stop

3mm bead

Silicon rubber tubing to length required pushed onto back of weight

Anti-tangle rig, abbreviated lead

18-inch rigid casting boom

Eye-tied hair-rigged boiled bait

Fixed lead weight

Hook trace of dacron, braided nylon or monofilament line, 2 or 3 inches overall shorter to the bait than the anti-tangle boom

Diamond-eye swivel

3mm bead

The rubber-tubed anti-tangle rig can be set up as the rigid rig is, using the same components for back stops, etc.

Fig 74   Long-range casting boom

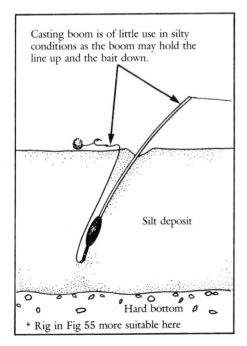

Casting boom is of little use in silty conditions as the boom may hold the line up and the bait down.

Silt deposit

Hard bottom

* Rig in Fig 55 more suitable here

Fig 75   Casting boom buried in silt

has other uses. The mounted-weight version is now made in a modular form to allow differing sizes of flexible boom tubing to be used, creating a more flexible system with fewer problems. The stiff-tubed booms can end up with the lead buried in the bottom or in weed (*see* Fig 75), trapping the bait as well as rendering the rig useless, although it is possible to reduce this by feathering the cast just before splash-down, as in Fig 76. The stiff boom can also hold the line up off the bottom, generating a possibility of line bites and false alarms as feeding, patrolling fish brush against the suspended line. To overcome this, weighted booms are now available from one manufacturer, Kevin Nash Tackle.

With all the various tackle arrangements and systems available it is possible to get tangles, and some experimenting with the rig will help you understand these and overcome them. It is possible to reduce and even eliminate them by fixing the hook and bait in

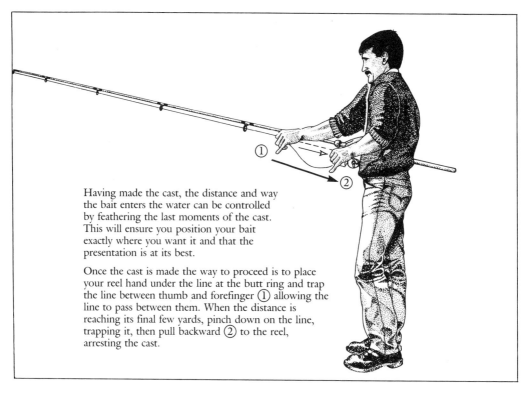

Having made the cast, the distance and way the bait enters the water can be controlled by feathering the last moments of the cast. This will ensure you position your bait exactly where you want it and that the presentation is at its best.

Once the cast is made the way to proceed is to place your reel hand under the line at the butt ring and trap the line between thumb and forefinger ① allowing the line to pass between them. When the distance is reaching its final few yards, pinch down on the line, trapping it, then pull backward ② to the reel, arresting the cast.

Fig 76   Feathering the cast to reduce impact

a position up the boom tube with PVA tape or PVA string, PVA tape being preferable as it will wrap around your bait better. This will dissolve shortly after settling on the bottom. The fixed hook and bait cannot then tangle before, during or after the cast. The value of the effort taken will depend on whether you think it is worth it.

Casting booms came into fashion because a need for them arose with the introduction of dacron hooklinks, etc., as outlined earlier. The casting booms will work equally well with nylon hooklinks and it is possible a lot of fish are becoming wary of the long black lines that point at the hookbaits. It is inevitable that the carp will become alarmed by black casting booms and black dacron hooklinks. Berkeley have introduced their camouflaged braided nylon to help overcome

this but you can also create your own by using white dacron. By colouring it with various coloured marker pens, the permanent ink types used in graphics studios and available from good office supplies shops, it is possible to make your line match exactly the sort of water you are fishing – multicoloured for shingle, beige for gravel, brown, green, whatever!

Another highly useful material is untreated dental floss which again is white and can be coloured in the same way. Perhaps somebody will come up with a camouflaged casting boom, or perhaps you have access to white plastic tubing which you can colour up. Give the idea some thought, and experiment when you notice some slowing down of interest by using a camouflage link or a monofilament hooklink with one of your rods. You might be surprised at the improvement; it is the difference that might just give you the edge over the other anglers on the bank.

Whatever you do with carp fishing do not get stereotyped for the sake of it, but observe the water closely and assess whether it will need margin, medium- or long-range tactics. Do not just chuck out to the horizon because everybody else does; check why they do it and then keep your eyes open. If a fish moves at closer range put a bait on its head – or almost! You will be fishing with at least two rods, so put one out with a different bait, a different rig or in a different area. When you have it right you can give the best area your undivided attention and reap the full rewards for your efforts.

7 Night Fishing

There are various reasons for night fishing but the two most obvious are the limit of time available during the week and the need to spend as much time as possible fishing at the weekend when there is no carp water nearby. Many carp anglers fish from the early evening into the night, possibly up to midnight or just after due to the pressure of having to go to work the next day. There are also many carp anglers who may not have a local carp water to fish during the week and who travel to their nearest water on a Friday evening to fish through Friday night to some time on Sunday. To maximise the results of the opportunity they will fish through both Friday and Saturday nights.

There is another reason for night fishing but this is one that possibly very few night-fishing carp anglers will have recognised yet. What most anglers come to observe during their longer fishing sessions is that more fish seem to fall to their baits during the periods of darkness. Depending on the type of water, there may be a logical reason for this, possibly daytime activity which has driven the carp out of range of the baits. If the water is day ticket and if limited night-fishing access is allowed to a small group of carp anglers, the carp may feel safe moving back into closer range to feed on all the free bait. This will provide easier fishing, but it is very rare to find a water where *all* the fish are caught after dark!

The angler who catches most fish after dark should observe whether the rest of the carp anglers are having the same results or are catching throughout the day as well. If they

are catching during the day this may indicate a possible shortcoming in the bait or terminal tackle of the angler who is only catching at night. It may be that the rig is too obvious, or it may not be presenting the bait as it should. Perhaps it is the wrong rig for the swim, or maybe the bait colour is too bright and obvious, particularly if it is one that has been well used and successful, to the point where the carp spook, simply on sight of it. The answer really, if this is the reason for your night fishing, is to take a long look at the terminal tackle and bait colour and try changing some aspect of the presentation. Observe the general appearance of the lake bed where it is visible. Clear water is another drawback and means your presentation must be natural. Coloured water, like darkness, takes the edge off the carp's visual sense letting you get away with poor presentation! If you have any doubt have a chat with a carp angler on your water, who is catching. He might point you in the right direction, but be careful not to make a nuisance of yourself.

A reasonably successful carp angler may encounter problems when he moves from a coloured water to a crystal clear water. He may have been successful with his bait and method because of the colour of the water but finds it hard to catch on the new water except after dark. If this happens to you, again take a look at your presentation and make adjustments. The results might astound you, so do not slavishly persist with a method because it caught elsewhere, as so many things vary from water to water.

A night-caught 16lb scattered-scale mirror carp from a gravel pit.

PREPARATION

The most obvious difficulty with night fishing is the lack of light to see what you are doing and where you are casting. Preparation for a night session must take place during the day or early evening to allow you to get your bearings. The degree of preparation can vary to suit the length of stay at the waterside. In this instance we will limit our preparation to cover a single overnight session. Once you have had some experience of that you can decide whether you would like to fish for longer and prepare yourself accordingly.

Dealing first with tackle and sundries, most of your tackle will be identical, but there will be a need to make your sundry items like spare terminal tackles, baiting needles and baits easy to find in the dark. One of the best ways to ensure this is to lay them all out on a white cloth or plastic sheet to one side of your fishing position. To help see what you are doing you should equip yourself with a small pocket torch or one of the clip-on flexible torches. Never use a large torch or Tilley-type lamp for too much light will disturb other anglers and create a blindness beyond the light of the lamp. Small spots of light will allow your eyes to readjust to the dark more quickly after use. Bite indicators will need some illumination; on bright moonlight nights simple white indicators will be reasonably visible but on dark nights you will benefit from fitting isotopes (Betalights) of a power of between 300 and 500 micro lamberts. These can be fitted into special sections of many of the purpose-made monkey climbers available in most tackle shops (*see* Fig 77). Terminal tackles can remain the same, and lines can remain the same or may be stepped up from 9 to 11 pounds (4–5kg) BS line to protect against snag damage.

Once you have chosen a swim you would be well advised to make some exploratory hook-free casts around to locate any possible snags, etc., and then make a mental picture of their location. Next, line up the point in the swim where you will position your baits; make a note of the background layout so you can line up with silhouettes of the background after dark. Then tackle up, cast to the exact point you wish to fish and make some mark on the line to indicate the exact distance to the spot for when you have to recast after dark (*see* Fig 78). This is a very important point to remember if you are casting to a bar, an island or the far bank margins, etc. There are several ways of doing this, for example by applying nail varnish to the line, or by wrapping an elastic band or strip of electrical tape around the line on the spool to trap it. It can also be useful in daylight!

With the nail varnish you can feel the line as it slips through your fingers and can then check the line travel by pinching down to stop it, reeling back any line to re-position the bait to the correct spot. With the elastic band or tape the cast will terminate with a slight jerk as the line comes up against it but with practice the strength of cast can be controlled to minimise the strength of the jerk, allowing smooth presentation. If correctly set with a few loops of line on the top, you can then set your indicators to whichever method you are using. With tape, use a narrow strip perhaps quarter of an inch (6mm) wide, set towards the back edge to allow line to be taken if necessary by a running fish.

With these key points organised, bait the swims you are going to fish and place your hookbaits in position. To gain the best position to deal with a run if it should come, set your seating close to your rods; a folding bed-chair is useful but can encourage you to relax too much with the risk of falling asleep. Bivvies should be used for longer sessions only, as they encourage you to be too far away from the rods. If you doze off in the

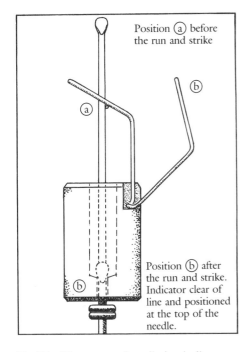

Position (a) before
the run and strike

Position (b) after
the run and strike.
Indicator clear of
line and positioned
at the top of the
needle.

Fig 77   Flip-top monkey climber indicator

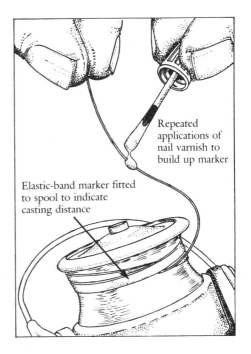

Repeated
applications of
nail varnish to
build up marker

Elastic-band marker fitted
to spool to indicate
casting distance

Fig 78   Marking distance on reel line with nail
varnish, etc.

warmth, you might not get to the rod quickly enough to stop a fish reaching a snag and end up injuring or losing the only fish of the session. The best way to fish is to sit beside the rods, as in Fig 79, prepared for the slightest activity that may occur. It can be tough but if you cannot stay awake or alert you should not be night fishing!

Organise the landing net either ready in the margin or stand it in a position of easy access should you hook a fish, lay out your unhooking pad in a suitable place and possibly lay out your weigh sling, scales and perhaps a keep-sack. All this will save a lot of hunting around in the dark.

With casts into tight areas where accuracy is vital make the final cast just before dark, to ensure a fresh bait is in position. Once it is in place you must leave it there until a take comes, as minimal casting will ensure minimal mistakes and tangles. If you have a take and need to recast, the markers will help

get it as near perfect as possible. A distinct advantage can be gained by using bait stringers at night to ensure your hookbait is near some free offerings. You can tie some up ready for use and store them separately.

That really takes care of the preparation advice except for mentioning the need for warm clothing, food and hot drinks to keep you warm overnight. It is surprising how cold it can get on a clear August night!

THE STRIKE

When a take comes, deal with the strike as normal and once in contact with the fish move close to the water and get down low so that you can see the rod silhouetted against the skyline; this will allow you to tell which way the fish is moving. Progress with the fight carefully and remember the positions of any snags, bars or obstacles. Once the fish is in

A beautiful, pearly-scaled mirror carp of 11lb from an estate lake fishery.

A sparkling, pristine example of a linear mirror carp of 14lb from Shillamill Lake in Cornwall.

At all times remain close to your rods to capitalise on any opportunity that may arise. If you must leave the swim for more than a few moments retrieve your baits.

Choose a comfortable chair and position it to allow you the best route to strike when you get a run, even from a sitting position.

Fig 79   Position close by rods

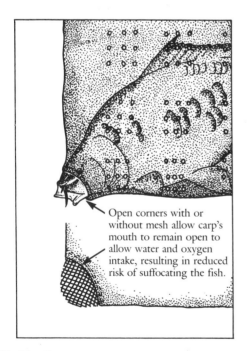

Open corners with or without mesh allow carp's mouth to remain open to allow water and oxygen intake, resulting in reduced risk of suffocating the fish.

Fig 80   Open corner keep sacks

close for netting lay the net out and gently coax the fish over it fully before lifting. At this point, refrain from using any light as this could spook the fish and cause you to loose it. Once it is netted, release the bail arm on the reel, lay the rod in the rod rests and then carry the fish to the unhooking pad. Unhook it quickly and, if you wish to weigh it, do so quickly. Then, depending on its size, release it or retain it in a suitable carp sack (*see* Fig 80), remembering to ensure it is upright. Check it regularly until you are ready to photograph it.

If you have followed all the advice you should get some good photographs and be able to return your fish safely and maybe give night fishing some extra effort in the future. But, remember, identify whether you are fishing at night for the right reasons, and you will probably enjoy your daytime fishing far more.

8 Handling and Fish Care

The current cost of carp is running at an alarmingly high level, with very high prices being paid for good quality fish. It seems very surprising therefore that more is not published on the subject of handling and fish care! Most articles or books on carp fishing seem to miss this particular point or, if it is discussed, the subject gets the briefest mention in the midst of a recollection of a memorable capture.

Maybe there should be some criticisms of the authors of carp articles and books but it is very easy to overlook the subject when you are trying to put over all the other points that make carp fishing what it is. To be fair, there is a current debate in the monthly magazines on the subject of injury and possible death of big carp from dangerous types of *fixed* bolt rig. If a breakage of the reel line above the fixed leger weight occurs, due possibly to the carp snagging the line or a breakage occurring during the cast, it leaves the carp trailing the bomb which may then become immovably snagged. The fish might be able to tear the hook free but with severe damage to itself or it may ultimately die from exhaustion and starvation. You should recognise that fish care begins with the method you employ to hook them. There is always a chance that something may go wrong and, as outlined in Chapter 6, you must ensure that rods and lines are balanced, that your line is in good condition and, when tying rigs, the knots are as strong as possible.

It is probably a good idea to discuss the subject fully to help the inexperienced carp angler and remind the forgetful experienced carp angler. In our excitement, we are all prone to an occasional lapse in concentration and may not always hook, play, land and handle fairly what might be the biggest fish in a given water or even the smallest; but they *all* deserve the same respectful treatment. On this point, let me say that it would be beneficial to *all* of us if every fish you capture, even the chance hooking of bream, tench, roach, rudd, etc., is also carefully landed, unhooked and returned undamaged as it is certainly not the fault of the fish! You placed the bait and hook out in their environment and know it is there for only the biggest carp in the lake to eat, but the fish do not realise this.

Before leaving this subject, do not get into the frame of mind where you cannot appreciate catching any fish smaller than your target, but stop and smell the roses along the way — fishing is about enjoyment! Those smaller carp you may swear about catching so often will most likely ensure that your reactions are finely tuned, so that when a really big carp takes your bait, you will be capable, due to your practice and experience, of playing and landing it successfully. You never know exactly what you have hooked until you get it into the landing-net. Many of us have thought we were playing just another small fish, only to find out it is over twenty pounds! So respect each fish you hook; you might just get a surprise the next time.

The rigs to avoid are those that cannot be shed if the line breaks, thus endangering the fish. These rigs are commonly known as bolt rigs and can be of the anti-tangle type or straight leger type as shown in Fig 72. The best way to fish is to use a semi-fixed lead bolt rig which can be seen in Figs 47, 49 and 63 in Chapter 6. The use of silicon rubber and power gum stop knots ensures that if a breakage occurs and the bomb becomes snagged, the fish can pull free and trail only a length of line, which should be removed at the next capture.

Balancing the tackle, with the rod's test curve matched to the correct strength of line, will help eliminate much of the risk of breakage and the loss of baited rigs. The use of tackle suited to the range you intend fishing at will also help prevent problems. At close range, a softer-actioned rod will prevent breakage on the line if a carp bolts during the fight (see Fig 83). Remember to check regularly that the clutch is freely operating; many anglers overlook or forget that conditions of climate, hot or cold, can affect the performance of the drag systems on most reels. You may set it just tight enough in the cool of the early morning only to find it does not give line in the heat of the midday sun, risking a breakage if the carp should bolt.

Fishing at long range again needs a balance in rod action and line to prevent a breakage

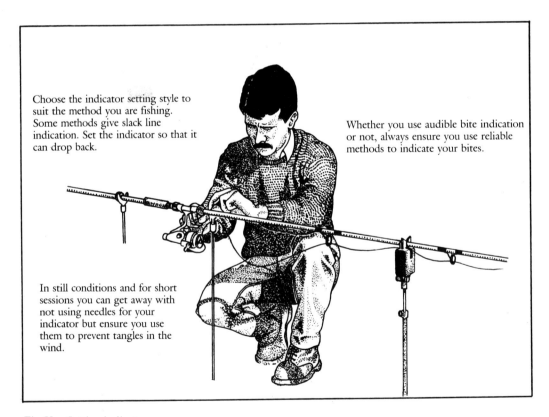

Choose the indicator setting style to suit the method you are fishing. Some methods give slack line indication. Set the indicator so that it can drop back.

Whether you use audible bite indication or not, always ensure you use reliable methods to indicate your bites.

In still conditions and for short sessions you can get away with not using needles for your indicator but ensure you use them to prevent tangles in the wind.

Fig 81 Setting indicators

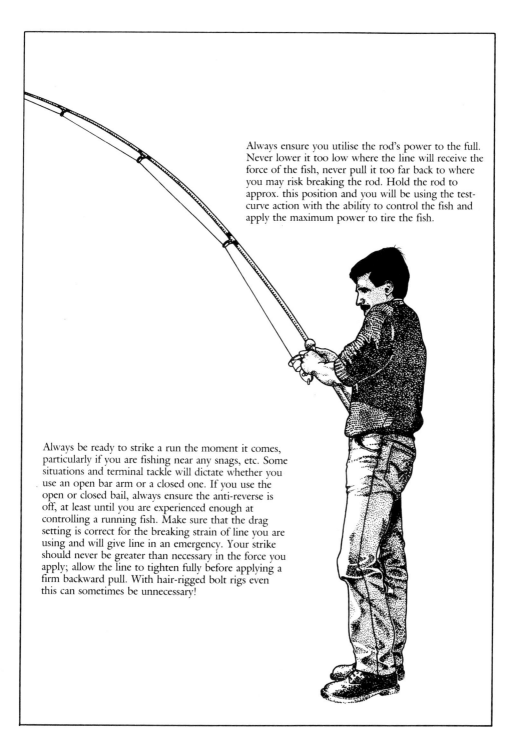

Always ensure you utilise the rod's power to the full. Never lower it too low where the line will receive the force of the fish, never pull it too far back to where you may risk breaking the rod. Hold the rod to approx. this position and you will be using the test-curve action with the ability to control the fish and apply the maximum power to tire the fish.

Always be ready to strike a run the moment it comes, particularly if you are fishing near any snags, etc. Some situations and terminal tackle will dictate whether you use an open bar arm or a closed one. If you use the open or closed bail, always ensure the anti-reverse is off, at least until you are experienced enough at controlling a running fish. Make sure that the drag setting is correct for the breaking strain of line you are using and will give line in an emergency. Your strike should never be greater than necessary in the force you apply; allow the line to tighten fully before applying a firm backward pull. With hair-rigged bolt rigs even this can sometimes be unnecessary!

Fig 82   Setting the hooks

In some situations it is more beneficial to apply side strain to control a
fish, when trying to turn it or tire it at close range, from the lower
position as illustrated. The important point to remember also is to use a
clutch setting which would just give line to a running fish or, once
experienced, back wind to give line.

Side strain has more effect on a fish than a high overhead pull. Side
strain can be applied to the opposite direction to which the fish may be
swimming.

Fig 83   Side strain at close range

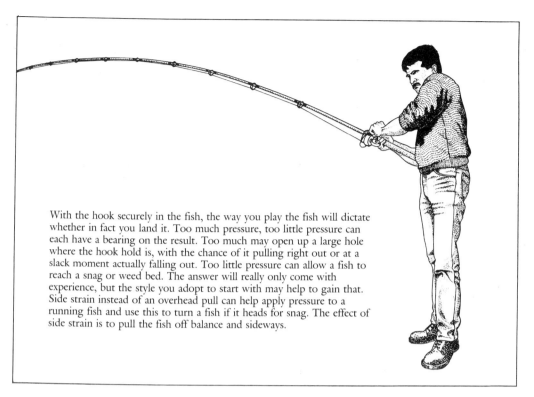

With the hook securely in the fish, the way you play the fish will dictate whether in fact you land it. Too much pressure, too little pressure can each have a bearing on the result. Too much may open up a large hole where the hook hold is, with the chance of it pulling right out or at a slack moment actually falling out. Too little pressure can allow a fish to reach a snag or weed bed. The answer will really only come with experience, but the style you adopt to start with may help to gain that. Side strain instead of an overhead pull can help apply pressure to a running fish and use this to turn a fish if it heads for snag. The effect of side strain is to pull the fish off balance and sideways.

Fig 84   Side strain at range

during the cast. The use of a shock leader of thirty feet of 15- or 18-pound line can assist here. It is also advisable when you are fishing over gravel bars, where the line is subjected to abrasion from stones and zebra mussels, etc., during the fight, risking a breakage of the line if the fish should spook and bolt from the landing-net. Finally, ensure the tackle you use is of sufficient strength to allow you to prevent fish from getting into snags, lilies, tree roots, etc., and to let you play the fish quickly to the net. There is no credit to be gained by playing a fish for thirty minutes to an hour. All you will be doing is expending the carp's energy and causing stress and a buildup of lactic acid which may cause severe distress and possible death from exhaustion. Be equipped to play the fish hard (*see* Fig 84) for the shortest period possible but take care

to play the fish with caution at close range, particularly with the stiffer long-range rods. Excessive force at the wrong moment may break your line or, worse, rip the hook and tear the fish's mouth. You may witness fish with split mouths during your fishing; they look horrible to us, and just think what the carp feels, so do take care.

Once you have played the fish to the margins and are about to net your prize, it is essential that the net is of sufficient size and of suitable material to land your fish (*see* Fig 85). To do this successfully you should have a triangular nylon-mesh net with arms of at least thirty-six inches in length. There is a type now available of two different meshes combined which allows for easy movement through the water due to a large-diameter side mesh, with a micromesh bottom section

Chris Turnbull uses great care in handling a beautiful fully scaled mirror.

Mike Woods gently lifts an evening-caught 12lb common carp from an estate lake, for photographing.

Once the fish is played out and ready for netting, either net the fish yourself or, if an experienced friend is with you, let him net it for you. This will allow you to concentrate on controlling the fish. The setting of the clutch is important: it must be able to give line or alternatively, once experienced, you can back wind should the fish spook on seeing you or the net. When playing the fish, never over-extend the time it takes to get the fish to the net; once hooked, play the fish as swiftly as possible. Too long may see the fish exhausted or the hook hold tear or weaken, causing the hook to fall out at the net or sooner!

Control the spool with your finger if required

Once over the cord of the net, lift the net to engulf the fish. Bring the fish to the net, never chase the fish with it!

Carry the netted fish away to the handling pad for unhooking as swiftly as possible.

36- or 42-inch arm, dual-mesh landing net.

Fig 85   Landing the fish

Before proceeding with any activity related to handling big or small fish, make sure you have taken every precaution to prevent the fish being damaged. This includes laying out a wetted handling mat on a soft bank, wetting the weigh sling and having all scales and forceps, etc., close at hand to reduce the time the fish is out of water.

Always have good quality scales available to get an accurate record of your capture.

Use a good quality weigh sling of adequate size to hold a large fish and always ensure the loops are long to prevent the fish being lifted too far above the ground.

Grassy area of bank

Always handle and weigh your fish on a handling pad as marketed by manufacturers like K.N. and E.T. Tackle, or something similar.

Fig 86   Weighing the fish over padding

Back she goes; a mid-20lb common carp is returned to a Cambridgeshire lake.

to support the fish after capture. The optimum size for a landing-net is probably one with forty-two-inch arms, big enough to land the largest carp we are likely to encounter in the UK.

Having netted the fish, you should now take the fish to a grassy area of bank to do the unhooking. If you are on a fishery where this is not possible for one reason or another, you should be equipped with a suitable handling pad. Two versions of this item are available commercially: from Kevin Nash Tackle or ET Tackle, the former being more durable with a foam filling. After placing the fish on the grass or the mat, ensuring no stones are about, swiftly unhook it and then place it – still in the landing-net – back in the margins while you prepare for the weighing (*see* Fig 86). If the fish is small and can be returned quickly, please do this.

A considerable number of anglers will fish into or through the hours of darkness. It is at this time that further consideration should be given to the safe handling of carp, from picturing in your mind all the snags around you and the layout of the net on grass or pad in darkness to the problem of retaining the fish until it is light enough for photographing. With today's camera technology there is no reason why good photographs cannot be taken at night, particularly with the medium-sized fish. Retention only risks fish loss. However, if you catch an exceptionally good fish or personal best you will probably want a really good photograph. Then you may well have reason to hold it until first light, and the only important thing to remember is to use the correct method to retain the carp. The obvious choice is a purpose-designed carp sack, with plenty of ventilation, and water circulation holes punched all over the material. It is also best to use a cornerless sack which will stop the carp jamming its mouth shut in the corner

and suffocating itself (*see* Fig 80). A recent innovation in fish retention is a keep tube, which is basically a sack supported by rings on the outside with access from slip clips at each end. Hopefully a good carp-sized one will soon be available. One point that should be remembered is *never* use a keep net for retaining carp – too much damage can occur to scales and fins.

With the fish in a suitable carp sack, proceed to place this in the deepest water possible and then support and check the fish is upright and stable. If everything is all right leave it in the darkness where it will usually lie quiet. You are best advised then to check the fish every half an hour to an hour to ensure that its condition is satisfactory. This is usually indicated by activity when you check with a small torch. If you notice anything is wrong get the fish out of the sack and into the landing-net or open water – you should not risk the health of the fish for your own ego!

If all goes well you should get your photographs as soon as there is enough light to work by; even use flash in the early light to improve the quality. You will probably wish you had taken the photographs at the time of capture because the moment you lift the carp sack out of the water your prisoner is likely to go berserk. With this activity in mind you should take every care to choose a soft area of ground and cover it with a handling pad or other padding to take the pictures. With all the camera equipment ready, proceed to remove the fish from the sack and get a secure hold on it immediately to prevent it wriggling and thrashing off the mat. A good move is to cover the fish's head with the sack to quieten it.

Once it is quiet, pick up the fish and place one of your hands around the wrist of the tail with the other around the snout, your palm underneath. A calming action is the placing of your index and/or middle fingers in the carp's mouth. It will tend to suck at them and this will allow you to raise the fish slowly. If you feel the fish is going to wriggle and thrash, put it down onto the mat and quickly cover it with the carp sack until it quietens down; then continue as before. You should kneel on the mat and lift the fish to only just above your knees, about level with your waist. Do not pose and play around with the fish but just get a few good photos on the bank, slip the fish back into the sack and take it down to a suitable piece of bank or margin, and maybe take a last shot of the releasing.

Once you are sure the fish is all right, slip it into the margins and gently support it until it swims off. Never retain fish unnecessarily, particularly during the daytime in hot conditions, and never hold fish just to accumulate a bag shot. Use the sack for retention overnight or preferably equip yourself with suitable camera gear to take photographs at night.

I hope I have been preaching to the converted, and that those who are new to carp fishing will help protect our fish. We have all tried to protect the fish for you to catch; now it is up to you to continue the effort for the future!

Useful Addresses

ASSOCIATIONS

(1) **The Carp Society**
33 Covert Road
Hainault
Ilford
Essex

(2) **Carp Anglers' Association**
Membership Secretary
Castle Cary Press
Castle Cary
Somerset

RECOMMENDED BAIT SUPPLIERS

(1) **Nutrabaits**
95 Main Street
North Anston
Sheffield S31 7BE
Tel: 0909 563597

Attractors, oils and base mixes, etc.
Available from tackle shops and direct.

(2) **Geoff Kemp Bait Ingredients**
Pilgrims Court
Days Lane
Pilgrims Hatch
Brentwood
Essex
Tel: 0277 74291

Ingredients, flavours and base mixes.
Available from tackle shops and direct.

(3) **Tony Osborne Particle Baits**
1 Morley Road
Sutton
Surrey SM3 9LN
Tel: 01-644 7747

Beans, nuts and seeds, etc.
Available direct only.

Suggested Further Reading

Bailey, J., and Page, M. *Carp – Quest for the Queen* (The Crowood Press)

Cacutt, L. *British Freshwater Fishes – The Story of their Evolution* (Croom Helm)

Clifford, K., and Arbery, L. *Redmire Pool* (Beekay Publishers)

Gibbinson, J. *Modern Specimen Hunting* (Beekay Publishers)

Hilton, J. *Quest for Carp* (Pelham Books)

Hutchinson, R. *The Carp Strikes Back* (Wonderdog Publications)
Rod Hutchinson's Carp Book (Hudson-Chadwick Publishing)

Maddocks, K. *Carp Fever* (Beekay Publishers)

Paisley, T. *Carp Fishing* (The Crowood Press)

Sharman, G. *Carp and the Carp Angler* (Stanley Paul)

Whieldon, T. *Carp Fishing (Fishing Skills)* (Ward Lock)

TECHNICAL REFERENCE MATERIAL

Andron, J. W., and Mackie, A. M. 1978. Studies on the chemical nature of feeding stimulants for rainbow trout. *J. Fish Biol.*, *12*, pp. 303–310.

Goh, Y., and Tamura, T. 1978. The electrical responses of the olfactory tract to amino acids in carp. *Bull. Jap. Soc. Sci. Fish.*, *44*, pp. 341–344.

Hara, T. J. 1976 Structure–activity relationships of amino acids in fish olfaction. *Comp. Biochem. Physiol.*, *54A*, pp. 31–36.

Hashimoto, Y., Konosu S., Fusetani, N., and Nose, T. 1968. Attractants for eels in the extracts of the short necked clam. (1) Survey of constituents eliciting feeding behaviour by the omission test. *Bull. Jap. Soc. Sci. Fish.*, *34*, pp. 78–83.

Hidaka, I., and Yokota, S. 1966. Taste receptor stimulation by sweet tasting substances in the carp. *Jap. J. Physiol.*, *16*, pp. 194–204.

Marui, T. 1977. Taste responses in the facial lobe of the carp. *Brain Research, 130*, pp. 287–298.

Pawson, M. G. 1977. Analysis of a natural chemical attractant for whiting and cod using a behavioural bioassay. *Comp. Biochem. Physiol.*, pp.129–135.

This material is available via your public library service from The British Library, Documents Supply Centre, Boston Spa, W. Yorks.

Index